COVID-19
HOUSE ARREST

BY RICHARD PLINKE

Bright
COMMUNICATIONS

Printed in the United States of America
Published in Hellertown, PA

Cover design by Dina Hall
Front cover photo by Patrick Shuck, FGX Creatve, LLC
Back cover photo by Terree Yeagle, The Moment Photography

Library of Congress Control Number 20209113292
ISBN 978-0-9888764-2-2
2 4 6 8 10 9 7 5 3 1 paperback

Bright
COMMUNICATIONS

Also written by Richard Plinke

From the Jaws of the Dragon:
Sales Tales and Other Marginally Related Stuff

More Droppings from the Dragon:
A Hitchhiker's Guide to Sales

Dancing in the Cave of the Dragon:
Adventures in the Wonderland of Sales

www.HowToSellThePlague.com

Dedicated to my Facebook Friends

You told me I helped you through the lockdown,

but it was the other way around.

Contents

Introduction

I own a sales training company named How To Sell The Plague, LLC. The name comes from a book I started writing 10 years ago called *How to Sell the Plague*. The name of the book comes from ... well, you'll have to read the book to find out. It's a memoir of my morphing from a college intellectual hippie to a professional salesman. I have the first two chapters done, but I've rewritten the third chapter 28 times. I think I'm almost there.

Meanwhile, I've completed and published four other books, including this one. I was committed to finishing *How to Sell the Plague* in 2020, and I was working diligently on that 29th revision when along came the coronavirus pandemic. People often refer to me as the Plague Guy, so I guess it was only natural that Melissa Draving, my assistant, suggested I use the Plague Guy moniker to write about the new plague. When I mentioned it to Deb Colitas, my web designer, she said I had to use crazy pictures like I did this past Christmas to help promote my last book, *Dancing in the Cave of the Dragon*. In that post, Melissa took a picture of me in a Santa outfit holding out my book while standing in the snow on my back deck. It got a lot of likes on Facebook and sold upwards of two or three copies.

I began writing these pieces 15 days after we were put on house arrest, and I posted five a week on Facebook, Monday through Friday — I tried to make it like a real job and keep some semblance of normalcy. The pictures accompanying each piece were very popular, more popular than my writing, I fear, so I've included them in this book. All but one were taken with my iPhone, and all props and costumes came from my closet and basement, except for a couple of items I bought at Target, a large corporation that sells everything that local, small businesses weren't allowed to sell.

Forty-eight blogs later ...

(Let me interrupt here to say I hate the word "blog." It sounds like a noise you make after five martinis on an empty stomach, leaning over the railing of the back door stoop to your neighborhood tavern; it sounds like the frenzied howl of a lunatic fringe nut pounding out his manifesto of non-sequiturious confusion; it sounds like the sound and the fury from a frustrated William Faulkner sitting in his basement in his underwear ... Okay, that's probably not a good one, but you catch my drift. Let's call them essays. That sounds more erudite, doesn't it? And for the record, my essays are not ravings and they're not sarcastic; they are provocative satire. And just so you know, provocative satire is ravings and sarcasm with a magna cum laude BA in English Lit.)

... you are holding in your hands the result of those two timely and prescient suggestions by Melissa and Deb.

Tuesday, March 16, 2020, will not go down in history as a day of infamy, but for millions of Pennsylvanians (and millions more across the country on various dates of incarceration), that's the day their lives were torn apart and many destroyed while being reduced to subjects with no constitutional rights, ruled by fiat from despots gone wild with power ... and looking for more. That's the day they closed most businesses, put tons of people out of work and ordered us to stay home. We were told the lockdown would be for only two weeks so that we could stabilize hospitals and supplies. Almost 12 weeks (81 days) later, we're finally out of jail but still in purgatory, awaiting the monarch's next morsel of freedom.

What a hoot those 12 weeks have been, giving me plenty of material, mostly about the systematic deconstruction of trust within our nation. All the haphazard guesswork, speculation and contradictory information we've been given from the most nonviable, treacherous sources — politicians, the media and bureaucrats — have created an environment of suspicion where it's hard to believe anything from anybody anymore.

And it just doesn't stop! This week Dr. Maria Van Kerkhove, head of the World Health Organization's emerging disease and zoonosis unit, said that asymptomatic transmission of the coronavirus is very rare.

OMG! You would have thought they found the body. The outcry from the guardians of misinformation was swift and deafening. I don't have the exact transcript of what was said to Dr. Van Kerkhove, but this is close:

WHO Ponderous Potentate: *"Are you out of your freaking mind?"*

Dr. Van Kerkhove: *"What'd I do?"*

WHO Ponderous Potentate: *"What'd you do? You just told the whole freaking world that we ruined their lives for no freaking reason, that's all!"*

Dr. Van Kerkhove: *"I was just telling the truth."*

WHO Ponderous Potentate: *"You want the truth? You can't handle the truth!"*

Dr. Van Kerkhove: *"What?"*

WHO Ponderous Potentate: *"The truth is what we say it is. Got that? Do you want to undo all the hard work we've done to scare the hell out of people so they'll do whatever we tell them to do? Do you? Huh?"*

The next day: **Dr. Van Kerkhove**: *"I was just kidding yesterday. I was* *being sarcastic. I'm a very sarcastic gal.*"

And so goes the merry-go-round. I know some folks who own an appliance store that didn't receive an exemption to stay open when the state issued its list of essential and nonessential businesses. In March, they wrote to the state asking for permission to stay open like the big box stores that sell appliances and like their main competition down the road, another locally owned appliance retailer that was allowed to remain open. After more than two months of not hearing a word from the powers that be, they went on a TV news program and told their story. Miraculously, the next day they got a call from the state informing them that their situation had been reviewed and that they would be receiving revised lists of essential and nonessential businesses the next day. When the lists arrived, my friends' store wasn't on either one.

There's only one takeaway from all of this: I am the only person left you can trust (and I'm not so sure about me).

Hope you enjoy the book.

Allentown, Pennsylvania
June 11, 2020

Day 15 of Captivity

3/30/20

So, I'm on Day 15 of my "We're All in This Together" experience and wondering how it is that we're all in this together.

I mean, I'm really in it, hunkered down in my hermetically sealed and fumigated basement office with all doors and windows bolted tightly so that no germs or money can get in and worrying about what's going to happen when the toilet paper runs out: *In my hour of need, I truly am indeed, alone again, naturally.*

Because I don't believe for a second that our fearless elected leaders and the quaffed and deodorized media are a bit concerned about wiping their own asses — not as long as they have us to do it for them. So, the real message in "We're All in This Together" is that you all, the great unwashed, should sally forth (or in this case, unsally unforth) to fight the good fight, and we'll be right behind you ... at a safe social distance, of course, which our armed and mean-looking bodyguards will enforce even if it means cracking a few Charmin-soft butts because we take this very seriously, and, if all goes well, we might win a Daytime Emmy.

Wouldn't that be swell?

Anyway, I used to get up at 5 a.m., wash up, shave, get dressed and sally forth to the gym. These days, I still get up at 5 a.m., wash, shave, get dressed and sally forth to the kitchen for my first breakfast of the day. This morning it was Cap'n Crunch. We were out of milk, so I poured some Arnold Palmer over the sweetened, yellow squares. We were out of bananas and blueberries, too, so I sprinkled on some Fritos and Cheez Doodles and mixed it all together. It wasn't as good as it sounds.

I was hopeful that Breakfast II would be better. In the meantime, I went down to my desk for a couple hours of work while snacking on almonds and raisins. You know, the kind encased in a protective coating of chocolate.

That's it for now. Enjoy your day and remember to wash your hands for as long as it takes to whistle the theme song from *The Bridge on the River Kwai*, a terrific film that will use up almost three hours of your day. I watched it yesterday between lunches. Unfortunately, I had to pause it in the middle for my midday snack.

Day 16 of Captivity

3/31/20

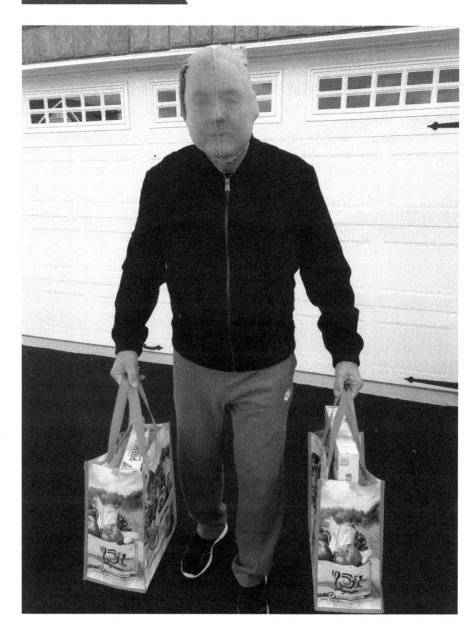

I read the news today, oh boy ...

I know, I know, I'm an anachronism, part of a dying breed who still reads newspapers. For millennials, that's a document containing a bunch of stories that were streamed and tweeted the day before and printed on cheapo, cheapo paper that gets cheapo-er by the day. It's really good stuff ... for putting under the canary's ass (as in, at the bottom of the bird cage to catch the droppings — a very old chestnut I first heard in Yellow Pages sales training as a good way to combat the competition of newspaper advertising — pretty sophisticated stuff, eh?).

No apologies for my jokes, folks. These are difficult times and we all must — well, most of us must — make sacrifices. So, ha, ha, right?

Anyway, in this golden age of fear and prejudice, the news, no matter the medium, is generally quite provocative, inflammatory and depressing, because *the name of the place is I like it like that.* Yeah, we like it; we like being mad as hell, only we're not going to stop taking it anymore. "Pissed off" is our battle cry; "Please Tread on Me" is our banner. We can't seem to get enough of the distorted, manipulated pablum being spooned out, bad news galore, packaged in bright shiny paper to catch our limited attention span, the more polished the turd the better. So, when something such as COVID-19 comes along, hip, hip hooray, strike up the band, happy days are here again.

Yay!

Okay, not yay, but pretty handy for infusing the masses with lots of fear and loathing. Like the body counts all the news outlets keep blasting at us, minute by minute: *Hey, don't worry, I've been lied to; I've been here many times before ... minute by minute by minute by minute I'll be holding on.*

Right on, right on; keep those numbers spinning exponentially as we collectively sit on the edge of our seats in front of the one-eyed monster waiting for the newest death tallies. It won't be long until Vegas is giving odds on the winning number: 100,000? 150,000? 200,000? 1.2 mil?

Jackpot!

Electrically, they keep a baseball score. And the beat goes on, the beat goes on.

I feel your pain, and in an altruistic effort to save you, body and soul, here are a few tips:

1. Use one of Zeno's paradoxes to practice social distancing. Zeno, the original practitioner of the scientific method known as reductio ad absurdum, postulated that motion is nothing more than an illusion because in order to reach a destination, you first must cross the halfway point to your destination. In order to reach the halfway point to your destination, you first must cross the halfway point to the halfway point of your destination. Then, in turn, you first must cross the halfway point to the halfway point to the halfway point of your destination, and so forth and so on … ad infinitum. Ergo, you can never go anywhere, so you might as well stay in place.

2. Practice safe sex. While copulating, refrain from all possible touching. You couples who've been together for a while already know how to do this.

3. Wash your hands after touching anything. Never touch your face. Touching other body parts is optional.

4. Vigorously wash your hands before and after applying hand sanitizer. When your hands dry out, crack and bleed, use hand cream. Be sure to scrub your hands after using hand cream.

5. Wear a mask. If you don't have a mask, put a nylon stocking over your head. You'll be surprised how quickly people get out of your way.

6. Try not to breathe.

4/3/20

I'm a 72-year-old man with a healthy prostate.

That may not mean much to you young whippersnappers, but to me and my peers it's a big deal. It's a big deal because it means I don't have to get up in the middle of the night to empty my bladder. That's right, folks, I sleep the whole night through, maybe not exactly like a baby but very much like a 72-year-old man with a healthy prostate. At least I did sleep through the night like a 72-year-old man with a healthy prostate until this troubling COVID-19 showed up with all its pervasive entanglements.

That may need some exposition. For some mysterious reason, in the past couple of decades, water has become the fix-all, cure-all, great-with-bourbon-and-a-twist-all elixir peddled by everybody from health experts to imaginative healers of all ilk. "Drink lots of water," they all say. It doesn't matter the ailment — you're tired, you're out of shape, you get headaches, you don't get headaches, you're too fat, you're too thin, you have hemorrhoids — plenty of water is the favored remedy to get you fit as a fiddle as you continuously piddle.

So, naturally, when the coronavirus reared its ugly head, my health care provider (who works out of a horse-drawn, festively decorated wagon) told me to drink lots of water.

"It cleans out your throat and esophagus and washes away the virus germs before they can take hold in your lungs," he preached.

Okay, so I've been drinking lots of water for the past two weeks and now I can't go more than 20 minutes without having to pee.

Talk about the cure being worse than the disease!

And speaking of miracle cures and urine, Indian politicians are offering an unusual remedy to keep the novel coronavirus in check. The Bharatiya Janata Party has suggested that cow urine is an effective disinfectant, and it could be used to cure COVID-19 by spraying it on people.

Really? I don't know about that. My wife says I've been spraying urine all over the place for years, and I don't think it's cured anybody of anything. It certainly hasn't cured her of nagging me about my aim.

But I'm working on my own cure for this insidious disease: Miller Lite. Willing to make any sacrifices for the good of mankind, I'm conducting thorough research into the brew's healing properties by drinking mass quantities every day (because it is mostly water, right?). And guess what? So far, it's working. I'm going to keep at it, and in another month or two, I'll let you know my findings. In the meantime, "Hiccup!"

Day 21 of Captivity

04/05/20

Here in Pennsylvania, the distribution of distilled alcohol is managed by the Pennsylvania Liquor Control Board, and you can only buy the hooch through an incestuous system of state owned and operated stores, fondly known as State Stores.

It's a really neat arrangement: The commonwealth makes a profit on all liquor and wine sold and then sticks a 6 percent vigorish (in the guise of a sales tax) on top of that.

And you thought we'd stamped out organized crime.

About two weeks ago, our interesting governor, Tom Wolf, announced he was closing all State Stores the next day because he didn't want crowds congregating in the stores. In all my years, I don't think I've ever seen crowds congregating in State Stores (even at Christmastime, when people seem to come and go rather rapidly) … until the Guv roiled the masses into action with his announcement. All hell broke loose as people jammed the stores, causing long lines to snake out the doors and onto the streets and parking lots.

As COVID-19 watched the whole fiasco with a smile on its face.

So, for our own safety, we can't buy liquor or wine in PA, unless, of course, you go to a grocery store such as Wegmans (my home away from home) where you may congregate in the wine section and buy as much nectar of the grape as you please, in the finest example of sophistry practiced masterfully by our often-confused leaders.

Yes folks, our Gov. Wolf is a real cut-up, and doesn't he do the darndest things, like the closing of all nonessential businesses that he and his minions had sole control in determining the viability of "essential." Unfortunately for Ol' Tom, a week after he ordered the shuttering of thousands of businesses across the state, spotlightpa.org reported that Wolf's former kitchen cabinet company did not shut down — it got a waiver to stay open.

Because we all know how essential kitchen cabinets are (for storing your liquor, if you could get any).

Then, after the media started asking questions, the waiver was rescinded. When asked about it, our dear, dear governor said, "Sometime they get it wrong."

What do you mean "they," Kemosabe? The problem is, you got it righ Mr. Wolf, because in today's political cesspool, taking care of your frienc and your own self-interest is business as usual. (The Kennedy Center comes to mind.) Your only mistake was getting caught.

I'll bet you could use a good, stiff drink at your favorite watering hol right about now.

Too bad you closed them, too.

04/06/20

You know what I miss most about all this? Going to the gym (and not because I miss the women in yoga pants, smart-ass — although I do ... somewhat desperately).

I miss the routine of getting up every day and working out, starting my day off with a vigorous and oxygen-rich workout (and yoga pants). I crave the discipline of setting a tone every morning for the rest of my day (and yoga pants). I need the workout to stay in shape and maintain good health (and yoga pants). I enjoy and take motivation from being around a bunch of people who are focused and dedicated (and ... oh, you know: Yo-ga! Yo-ga! Yo-ga! ... We *might as well have a good time* [and almost nobody's going to get this one!]).

Working out at home isn't the same, especially since I've spent the last couple of years divesting of all my work-out equipment: Universal machine, bench, full set of barbells up to 70 pounds and various and sundry other items of self-abuse. I hadn't used any of the gear in years since I discovered the benefits of yoga ... er, I mean the gym. I figured I'd never again need the stuff.

Who knew?

So I'm doing push-ups, sit-ups, leg lifts, leg curls and lots of stretching. Additionally, I'm adding pull-ups to my repertoire. I've seen men and women doing them at the gym, and I always wanted to try a couple, but I didn't want to embarrass myself — I know how hard they are from my football days. I'm using one of my son's discarded P90X pull-up bars that I found buried in the basement. I didn't need any hardware or tools to hang it; it wedged into a doorway and stays leveraged in place — it's a pretty cool device. I'm using a small step stool, too, to stand on and help with lift. It's going well, and I figure if I keep at it, I'll be able to do one by the time the quarantine is lifted.

Also, I take my dog for lots of walks and ride my bikes most days. I have a road bike, a trail bike (hybrid) and a mountain bike (with really cool three-inch tires that are great in the snow!). I don't like riding my road bike much anymore because it's become hazardous out there.

People seem so angry these days, and I make a great target alongside the road. You'd be surprised how many times I've been run at or almost hit. I've grouped those dangerous drivers into three categories: Trump supporters who think I'm a communist because my bike and all my equipment and clothing are made in China; Bernie supporters who don't like my relatively expensive bikes because everybody can't have one; and Biden supporters who are usually asleep at the wheel.

Accordingly, I pretty much stick to the myriad trails we have winding through the Lehigh Valley, although they've become so crowded with folks suffering from cabin fever that I have to be careful. I wear full-length biking pants, socks and shoes, a turtleneck, jacket, gloves, a full head and face cover, goggles and helmet. No part of my body is exposed, and when I get home, I take a Lysol shower.

Not everybody's as careful, though. I see people with exposed mouths, noses, eyes and all kinds of skin. Some of them are holding hands. That's nice — maybe they like to share everything. I saw one couple walking arm in arm, and they both had on headsets. There they were, strolling through Pennsylvania's pastoral beauty and listening to what I can only assume were different tunes. They looked very happy, and that got me thinking: I bet I'd get along a whole lot better with my wife if I wore a headset all the time.

Day 23 of Captivity

04/07/20

We're a long way from home. Welcome to the Pleasuredome.

The one thing I've learned for certain from COVID-19 is that "expert" means maybe, could be, might be, not a clue, probably not. And boy, don't we have the experts coming at us fast and furious. If you believe these interlopers, the pandemic will be over in four weeks, two months, six months, a year, never, what epidemic? And 50,000 people will die, 100,000 will die, 200,000 will die, 1.5 million will die, everybody whose last name begins with an M, an E, an N, a D, an A or an X, plus all those dissemblers with one name, will die. My prediction is that everybody will die … eventually.

So, I guess I'm the only real expert here. Yeah, let's go with that.

As an expert, my prediction is that the media will trip all over itself for the duration of the epidemic with deliberately frightening half-truths and reckless speculations while disseminating the most irresponsible claptrap and useless nonsense packaged as learned insights. Here's my favorite so far this week: NBC News reports that Dr. Robert Redfield, director of the CDC, told NPR that as many as a quarter of his patients are asymptomatic.

Huh?

Asymptomatic means they have no symptoms, and if they have no symptoms, why are they patients? And why is the CDC (Centers for Disease Control and Prevention) wasting time with people with no symptoms?

"Well, you know, they tested them," you say.

Okay, if that's the case, why are they testing people with no symptoms? Look, I'm sure there are folks out there with the flexibility of Gumby who can twist meaning out of any irrationality (have you been watching the debates?), but this concept just boggles the mind.

Almost as much as to mask or not to mask, that is the question. It makes sense to wear a mask, and, since I'm the expert, I say wear a mask. If you don't have a mask, wear a scarf or a turtleneck or anything that will cover your mouth and nose to help retard the passing and receiving of germs. (I saw one ingenious soul use of a pair of men's underwear, so free your imaginations.) The debate is stupid. See how easy things are when I'm in charge?

There is one other guy I recommend listening to, and that's Vice Admiral Jerome Adams, the U.S. Surgeon General. He's a bright young man who seems to be immune to hysteria and hyperbole (which makes you wonder how he got the job, right?). While many of the talking heads with titles in front of their names give us daily scoldings for being bad boys and girls, Dr. Adams says positive things such as, "Most people across the country are doing the right thing. Ninety percent of the country is staying home." He has some other wild ideas, too, like, "More people will die, even in the worst projections, from smoking cigarettes in this country than are going to die from the coronavirus this year."

Wow! That's practically blasphemy. He better get with the program if he wants to stay on TV. As an expert, my advice to Dr. Adams is to say stuff like: *Mine is the last voice that you will ever hear. Do not be alarmed.*

04/08/20

One of the most common things said by people who've contracted COVID-19 is that they've lost their appetites.

So, if you're wondering how I'm doing, no worries in that area. Unfortunately.

When they start telling us that eating like a horse is a symptom of the disease, I'm going straight to the emergency room, posthaste!

Because I haven't stopped eating in, (what's it been now?) three weeks? A month? A blue moon? Who can keep track between making meals, disinfecting the counters and the dog and running the dishwasher? (And if you want to make some money after the lockdown, take a YouTube course on dishwasher repair.) I've stopped labeling my feedings because now that the days are longer and we're stuck inside, it's become almost impossible to differentiate between morning, noon and night. It's always now o'clock on some unidentified day of the week, so I figure I might as well eat.

And eat I do, to the point that I tried on a pair of jeans this morning, and WHOA, FREAKIN' JACK! They really shrunk.

Or something.

I don't get it because I've disciplined myself to eat only good, solid foods from the basic food groups. Here's a sample of my food intake per food group. You be the judge.

1. I like to have a half-dozen or so slices of crispy fried bacon (protein) with my fried eggs (dairy) and fried hash browns (vegetable). When you throw in buttered toast, you get grain and more dairy. (I'm way ahead already.)

2. I might have some blueberries (fruit) for a snack with maybe a little whipped cream (more dairy — I'm kicking ass on dairy).

3. I like tuna (protein) on sourdough bread (grain) with gobs of cheese (dairy — I've really got this category going, don't I?) melted in the oven. As you well know, you can't eat tuna fish without

potato chips (vegetable).

4.   I like to have some pretzels (grain) for another snack, especially the stick kind that is so good at scooping ice cream (dairy, my old friend) right out of the carton, chocolate, of course (vegetable — what? cocoa beans grow out of the ground, you know).

5.   There's nothing like a thick, sizzling steak (protein) with deep-fried onion rings (vegetable), a baked potato (vegetable) dripping with oozing butter (OMG, dairy), and a side salad (vegetables galore) full of croutons (grain). I like to have a little wine (fruit) with my steak, maybe a bottle or two (lots of fruit).

6.   For a nosh, I enjoy popcorn (vegetable) with melted butter (even more dairy, can you believe it?) and prodigious amounts of beer (prodigious amounts of grains).

As I mentioned, this is only a sampling; I'm getting many more of these vital nutrients every day, too numerous to elucidate. Lots and lots of them. So, you tell me: What's the problem? I'm scratching my head. Maybe I'm not getting enough of this sustenance; maybe I need to eat more.

Go figure.

4/9/20

You don't have to call me darlin', darlin.' You never even called me by my name.

This is one of my favorite lyrics in all of musicdom because I've felt like that a good part of my life. Haven't we all?

The song was written by Steve Goodman and made famous by David Allen Coe. Although the person who inspired it, who came up with that great line in the chorus, who first recorded it and then sat on the sidelines as other people got famous, as so many did, covering his own songs — was John Prine.

John Prine died on April 7 from bad health, aided by COVID-19. He was only 73.

The depressing coverage of the coronavirus keeps coming at us, and *all the news just repeats itself, like some forgotten dream that we've both seen.*

That is, until it gets personal.

I didn't know John Prine, but I knew his music, or should I say, my music, because like all art, as soon as the artist puts it out there, it's no longer his or hers; it belongs to the audience, in a very personal and individual way. Although John Prine is dead, his music is very much alive, and, for me, will not die until I do.

Prine and I had some interesting similarities: We were both products of the '60s with all the associated chaos and colliding and disorienting messages; we both worked for the post office, delivering mail for a couple of years; we both had squamous cell cancer, his on the neck, mine on the tongue; and we both endured six weeks of radiation treatments. After he went through his, he didn't do much for some time because I guess he felt that *sweet songs never last too long on broken radios.*

When Prine came up in the early '70s, he was touted as the next Bob Dylan. I thought that was an unfair comparison for anyone because Dylan was unique, just like Prine turned out to be. And other than playing guitar and singing with gravelly voices born out of the Woody Guthrie tradition, I didn't think they were that much alike. I think of Dylan as an esoteric, opaque impressionist and Prine as an in your face, reality storyteller. Apparently Dylan saw the difference as evidenced by once saying that "Prine's stuff is pure Proustian existentialism." That may not mean much to you, but for an old English major, it's a tingle up the leg.

This ugly pandemic creeps closer to home and takes with it not just the nameless few, but a life story in each victim. These are sad days for some, but for the rest of us, we're just trying to get by.

So, I'll keep laughing and hoping for the best. And as for John Prine, *hello in there.*

Day 28 of Captivity

4/12/20

A sadder man but wiser now I sing these words to you.

We're being careful around my house: My wife and I are practicing social distancing … for several years now.

And no place am I more careful than when I go to the grocery store. Even in non-coronavirus times, I'm careful of all the microbes floating through the air and hitching rides on carts and food stuffs. I mean, can you imagine a better incubator for nasty germs just waiting to enrich their circle of influence? I can't. That's why I always disinfect the handle on my shopping cart and thoroughly wash produce when I get home.

Like lemons. I use a lot of lemons in my cooking, but buying them gives me the creeps. Did you ever watch someone picking out lemons? They always have to touch and examine every one in the bin, like they're weighing them for gold content or something. That's why I soak my lemons in bleach. Sure, they taste a little funny, and sometimes I can't remember my name or how many toes I have, but better safe than sorry, right?

I've mentioned before how much I like going to Wegmans, and under normal circumstances, I go there almost every day. One of the reasons I go there almost every day is that I love their freshly baked muffins, the ones made from whole wheat (as opposed to half wheat, I suppose) with cranberries and walnuts — mmm, mmm good! and practically healthy.

So when the draconian and seemingly arbitrary (because, outside of a hospital, you probably can't find a better place to get you some COVID-19 than at a grocery store) measures were enacted, they stopped making my favorite muffins. When I asked why, I was told that they weren't baking any individual products on racks so that people wouldn't be touching them and spreading the virus.

"What about the lemons?" I asked.

"Lemons are in produce," she said.

"I know," I said. "And in produce you can touch anything you like."

She looked at me like I had two heads.

"What's the difference?" I asked.

"That's store policy," she said and shuffled off.

A week later, I was lucky enough to find a thermometer, the last one in the store. It was one of the new kinds that doesn't use mercury. It was fat like a thin cigar and slippery, so I had a hard time keeping it under my tongue. It just wasn't ergonomically designed, and it kept slipping out of my mouth. One day when I was sitting at the kitchen table taking my every-15-minutes temperature, it slipped out and crashed to the floor. It's a good thing it didn't have any mercury, as all I had to deal with was cleaning up the itsy-bitsy microscopic pieces of glass.

Which I did and carefully put all the itsy-bitsy microscopic pieces of glass back in the container and took the cellularly reconfigured thermometer back to Wegmans, along with the receipt, of course. The woman at the customer service counter told me I couldn't return the cellularly reconfigured thermometer until the end of April.

"Excuse me?" I asked, incredulously.

"No returns until the end of April," she repeated.

"Why?" from still incredulous me.

"Because you touched it," she said, inexplicably. "We're trying to prevent the spreading of germs."

"But I touched it before your clerk rang it up and then put it in the bag and then handed it to me. I breathed on it before he touched it, and then he breathed on it before he gave it back to me. As a matter of fact, I breathed on him, and he breathed on me, and the whole store was engaged in breathing all over each other in a breathing orgy, just like I'm now breathing on you and you're breathing on me."

She looked at me like I had two heads.

"That's store policy," she said.

I was paralyzed in disbelief for a moment, then asked, "Do you know in what aisle they keep the pretzel logic?"

She thought for a moment and then said, "I don't know; let me look it up," and started to type.

"Never mind," I said. "I think I found it."

I threw the thermometer in a trash can on my way out.
He said, you must be joking son, where did you get those shoes?

Day 29 of Captivity

4/13/20

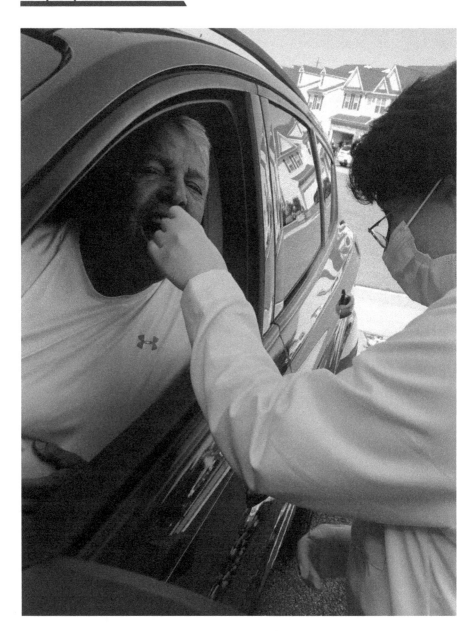

You know how much I like going to Wegmans, so when I showed up yesterday morning, I was disturbed to find people lined up on both sides of the building waiting to get in.

Apparently, they were only allowing a certain number of people in the store at one time. The lines were long and the social distancing was maybe four feet, three feet in some cases. Better than letting the irresponsible and rein-free horde into the store to disperse within the three million square feet of Wegmans normal footprint where social distancing is generally, at worst, four feet. We all must do our part, even when it makes little sense to the uneducated and uninformed hoi polloi. I mean, who the hell are we to think we should be treated like adults when it's obvious that the oligarchy knows best?

Thank God for the oligarchy.

As an example of that benevolence, one very minor member of the oligarchy, Pennsylvania State Rep. Mike Schlossberg, posted on Facebook some COVID-19 stats that the commonwealth had released, followed by the statement, "If you think this is fake or overwrought, or that social distancing isn't working and needs to end, defriend me now. Right now. On the spot."

Nice.

Singing songs and carrying signs. Mostly say, hooray for our side.

And please don't interpret any of this as a lack of seriousness on my part regarding the virus — seriously, folks, I take it seriously. I take it so seriously that I got tested.

You see, I had been tired for a couple of weeks, I had a sore throat, a dry cough, the sniffles and shortness of breath. My wife insisted that I be tested. She wanted me to be tested so badly that she sat me down and made me call my doctor for a FaceTime virtual visit.

I thought it was rather odd that she went into the next room soon after my visit concluded, where I could hear her on the phone with our life insurance guy. What could she possibly be talking to him about at a time like this?

During the visit, I told my doctor that every year at his time I get a sore throat, the sniffles and a dry cough from allergies — the Lehigh Valley syndrome, pollen galore every spring trapped between the mountain range to our south and the mountain range to our north, a veritable festival of sneezing, sniffling, coughing and blowing your nose until it looks like Rudolph's.

I didn't even know I had sinuses until I moved here.

"Do you have a fever?" my doctor asked.

"No."

"How do you know?"

"Because my wife makes me take my temperature about every 15 minutes. She can be very nasty about it," I added. "Especially when I'm done — she's very concerned and diligent about my temperature."

"What about this shortness of breath?" he continued.

"Well, I do have trouble with that … every time I exercise," I told him.

He decided to have me tested to be on the safe side because I'm high risk. In a nutshell, I'm high risk because I'm not dead yet.

Accordingly, I drove through a tent in the parking lot of a medical center close to my home, where they swabbed the back of my throat and gave me a lecture on COVID-19 proper behavior. Basically, the lecture boiled down to: Don't do anything.

It took only 24 hours to get the results, and I found my wife in the bedroom going through my closet and making notes (for what I don't have clue) and gave her the news.

She looked at me for a moment with a pained expression on her face and then started to cry.

"That's great news," she said almost inaudibly through the tears, her voice cracking.

She was so happy she could barely contain herself.

Day 30 of Captivity

Give me a head with hair, long beautiful hair, shining, gleaming, streaming, flaxen, waxen. Give me down to there hair, shoulder length or longer.

No, not anymore. Actually, I need a haircut … desperately.

And I could probably use a shave, too. If something doesn't break soon, I'll end up looking like I did in the accompanying picture, taken recently (recently being a relative term). In this particular case, recently was 1972. OMG, I'd never want to look like that again, right?

Are you in the same boat? I don't know if we all are, though, because I see Andrew and Chris Cuomo on TV every day and neither of them looks like they need a trim; it looks like they're still regularly getting their hair cut, and Chris is quarantined in his basement.

How does that work?

I see the talking heads and all of our elected officials from Washington on the 24/7 cable news outlets, and none of them are starting to resemble Lon Chaney, Jr., either. Even the man of the hour, Dr. Anthony Fauci, looks neat and clean, like he was *drinking a piña colada at Trader Vic's, and his hair was perfect.*

I don't have a clue what President Trump does to his inexplicable hairdo (or more appropriately, hairdon't), but I'm sure he has a full-time hairologist on staff to sculpt and lacquer his coiffure daily. And then there's poor Boris Johnson (who you don't hear much about now that he apparently won't be sleeping with the fishes), who obviously could care less about his hair.

But I guess the most inexplicable of them all is Tom Hanks. Did you see him on *Saturday Night Live?* His head was shaved almost to the scalp. He claimed it was from a movie he was working on, but he's been quarantined since March 11. In other words, he's telling us his hair hasn't grown appreciatively in 34 days.

Really?

I don't know. Hanks and his wife, Rita Wilson, have a combined worth of about a half-billion bucks, so I just can't believe Tom didn't get a little fix-up before the show, and I can't picture Rita grabbing the shears with a number one guard, sitting Tom down on a stool in their middle-class, suburban kitchen and going to town on a head that's probably insured for millions.

And that kitchen is smaller than the one in our townhouse. Yeah, I'm not buying that either. I'll bet it's a kitchenette attached to the master bedroom suite, or they shot the scene from the live-in help's quarters — very staged-looking, typewriters and all. Hard to believe a big Hollywood type such as Tom Hanks would try to deceive us.

But hold on there a minute, stow away that cynicism and remember, "Together we can beat this thing," or at least that's what the celebs and jocks keep telling us on all those groovy TV commercials. The only problem is, I'm a few million short of that kind of togetherness. No, my kind of togetherness involves Hamburger Helper and cleaning the toilets. Hey, if you guys want to experience real togetherness, come on over and grab a brush and the Lysol, after which I'll prepare for you an epicurean feast of Cheesy Beef Pasta. Just remember to please wear a mask and gloves … but you'll probably want those gloves anyway.

How bored are we?

Or stupid?

Hard to tell the difference because the inanity keeps coming at us faster and in greater quantity than COVID-19 briefings.

What happened to the great American innovators who put men on the moon and gave us pop-up Pez dispensers? Where's that limitless, creative inspiration that drove this country from an untamed wilderness (discounting the millions of Native Americans who got in our way) to rush-hour traffic jams (or in the case of California, 24/7 traffic jams)? Where are the movers and shakers who brought us high-def, surround-sound entertainment centers right in our own homes and then programmed modern-day Shakespearean gems such as *The Real Housewives of Beverly Hills* and *The View*?

Well, don't worry folks, that spirit is alive and well on Facebook, home of Big Brother and mesmerizing banality designed to make the transition to obedient scullions seamless. You hardly even notice as they deftly remove your cerebrum and replace it with uncomplicated group think. Don't believe it, eh?

I spy with my little eye ...

Wasn't it Sir Isaac Newton who invented that game?

Okay, I'll play. I spy with my little eye ... a bunch of drooling dunderheads with way too much time on their hands.

Try reading a book instead — perhaps a book with a cool dragon on the cover? (Just a thought, and by the way, I'll be holding a Zoom book signing event next week. Stay tuned for details.)

If you don't like that game, how about this one: List seven famous people you have met and make one a lie.

1.   Sir Isaac Newton
2.   Gene Rayburn
3.   Humpty Dumpty
4.   Jim Rockford
5.   Cheech & Chong (Does that count as two?)

6. Sam-I-Am
7. The one and only Billy Shears

Here's another one of my favorites — give yourself one point for each thing you've done:

1. Ridden in a limo
2. Driven a limo
3. Seen a picture of a limo
4. Rollerbladed
5. Rollerbladed twice
6. Never rollerbladed but said you did
7. Boot hopped (add 10 bonus points if you know what that is)
8. Broken a bone (add one bonus point for each broken bone)
9. Broken someone else's bone (add one bonus point for each person)
10. Skipped school
11. Went to school
12. Been on TV
13. Watched TV
14. Been to New York City
15. Been to Europe
16. Been to Uranus
17. Ridden a horse
18. Ridden a cow
19. Milked a cow
20. Milked a horse (not you, Catherine the Great — block that one out for the young 'uns)

Add up your score and subtract an equal number from it. Then add the number of minutes you spent reading this provocative essay. The sum of that equation is the exact number of minutes you'll never get back.

Haven't had enough yet, eh? How about some advanced Facebook activities, like the "In the Air Tonight" challenge where you slam shut your kitchen cabinets to the drum beat of Mike Tyson's favorite part of the song: "da-da, da-da, da-da, da-da, da-da dum, crash." Only with cabinets, it's more like slam, slam, slam, slam, slam, etc.

Have you tried the handstand challenge? If you do, there's a good chance you can answer number eight above with a point. But not Simone Biles, the world champion gymnast, who took it to a new level when she removed a pair of sweatpants while standing on her head.

Look ma! No hands.

Big deal. I can eat an entire bag of Oreo cookies while lying flat on my back on the couch, and I'm talking the 19.1-ounce family pack! Let's see Simone try that with her tiny little belly.

That's my kind of challenge.

Day 32 of Captivity

4/16/20

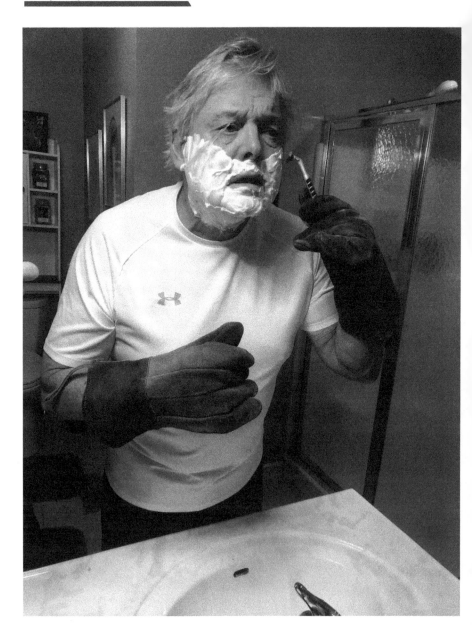

It gets harder every day to get up in the morning.

I lie in bed trying to decide whether to watch reruns of *Law and Order* and *Gilligan's Island* or get out from under the covers and face the incessant ghoul count and relentless pummeling of public service execrations. Then I stand in front of the bathroom mirror for five minutes deliberating whether to shave or not, which has become a rather difficult task without, you know, touching my face and all. I did, however, see a helpful tutorial on YouTube where a guy with a beard demonstrated how to shave using a paint roller and selfie stick. Next, I do a Franklin T-Chart on the wall using my wife's lipstick regarding the merits of showering, and the pro side always seems to have the last word with the scent factor (although that seems to be less and less a consideration).

When I finally get downstairs, I have to deal with the issue of food. No, not the consuming thereof — I'm real good in that area — but the restocking thereof.

Which requires a trip to the grocery store.

Which requires getting dressed in something other than pajama bottoms.

Which requires putting on some kind of legitimate footwear.

Which requires combing my hair (and it's a good thing I took a shower or I'd have no problem maintaining government-approved social distancing — hey, I have an idea …).

Which requires driving the car (which has become a strenuous exercise).

Which requires putting on a mask and gloves (which make my face and hands sweat and there goes the benefits of showering, and hello, social distancing).

Oh, what a bother. The alternative is to veg out in bed and call Melissa Draving of *Here For You Concierge* to go to the store for me and do my shopping, which I recommend wholeheartedly at *www. hereforyoupa.com* (and what a ridiculously obvious product placement — or service placement, in this case — which probably has you wondering,

"Hey, Rich. What's in it for you?" Just the warm feeling of helping out a friend during these difficult times … *and a few other things.*

I suppose many of us are having discipline problems, but fortunately, emails, Facebook and LinkedIn are helpfully providing us with all kinds of advice and systems to remain focused, productive and happy. And all for free because we're the most altruistic bunch of swell people you'll ever want to meet.

Speaking of free stuff, remember the old price-versus-value formula. So, in that spirit, here's my free advice for getting through these trying times:

1. Forget being focused and productive. Nobody cares if you're focused and productive. All they care about is their next meal.

2. Forget being happy. None of us is happy. Be satisfied with a warm feeling.

   Hope that helps.

4/19/20

I think we've reached a draconian level on using the word "draconian."

And it really pisses me off!

It was one of my favorite words (and I even knew what it meant and its derivation before you could Google words and learn just enough to misuse them), but now it sounds hackneyed. Of course, a little thing such as "hackneyed" has never stopped me. For those of you who regularly read my stuff, you know that my style (and yes, I have a style, wisenheimer) tends to lend itself periodically to the well-trod (because it's easier than thinking up new stuff all the time), and some of you might even think it's part of my beguiling charm.

Another rhetorical misappropriation you may be getting tired of is "statistical analysis." Mark Twain, along with a plethora of others, has been credited with defining the three types of lies: lies, damn lies and statistics. Do you ever wonder why the weather people can call 10 out of four storms? Statistical analysis. This may come as a shock to some of you, but there are no facts when dealing with future events. Weather forecasting is based on taking historical data and statistically figuring out probabilities. Those predictions are basically based on an average of past weather, and, unfortunately for the excitable meteorologists (who live for big weather events), those averages hold some wild swings within them. The chaos theory informs us that those anomalies are as predictable as the statistical probabilities.

It's all very confusing, but here we are in the midst of a singular and uncharted pandemic where anybody with a pulse, from dubious experts to obtruders with access to the internet, can predict future events without any historical data, which means they have even less chance of being on target than the weather folks. But don't despair: Luckily, we live in a time of flexible statistics, like last week when New York added 3,778 people who had never been tested for COVID-19 to its death totals. It just assumed the poor souls had the coronavirus.

If that's the new governmental normal, then the next time the IRS asks me if I paid my taxes, I'm going to tell them that I assume I did.

And what exactly is the "new normal," anyway? I bet the same linguistics genius who coined that one also originated "tap the brakes," "it is what it is" and "at the end of the day."

Banality galore!

I don't have a clue what the new normal is. If it means a normalization of social distancing and better adherence to personal hygiene, I don't think so. It won't be long until we're offering limp, sweaty or vice-grip handshakes to one and all, hugging people whether they like it or not and spitting all over each other when we talk.

If the new normal is buying as much toilet paper as we can find, eventually it's going to run out. Then we'll have a real mess on our hands. Do you think toilet paper grows on trees?

Like money does in Washington? If you think the new normal is the Band of Thieves giving us money, ha! In a classic con game, this step is called "putting up the mark." Welcome aboard, mark.

In Pennsylvania, I think the new normal is that we're now mushrooms. What else could we be? The governor keeps us in the dark and feeds us nothing but manure. (Hackneyed, I know — don't say you weren't warned.)

Maybe the new normal means we're going back to the time of Marie Antoinette, only instead of cake, let them eat $13 pints of ice cream.

Speaking of ice cream, you know what the real new normal is? Men wearing 40-inch, stretchy-waist pants and women in size 20 smocks. The real new normal, fellow cave dwellers, is stuffing as many calories into your mouth as you can with no guilt or remorse because we're all in this together.

Blimps galore!

Yes, we're all in this together, as we learned on Saturday night's "*One World: Together at Home*" extravaganza. And what we learned was that we all must make sacrifices for the good of humanity — I mean, some of these stars (not you, Keith Richards) haven't been able to get a Botox shot for over a month.

Oh, the humanity!

And in this age of social distancing, please explain how they got that grand piano onto Elton John's driveway?

Incidentally, all you hoopsters who haven't been able to play because they've shut down the playgrounds, hop on over to Elton's house for a game of horse. He has two basketballs, so no waiting. I'm sure he'll be happy to see you because we're all in this together, right?

FYI: Draconian comes from Draco, a legislator in ancient Greece who

set up arbitrary laws with harsh penalties. Eventually, the Athenians h
enough of Wolf's … er, I mean Draco's unilateral and punitive rules a
drove him out of Athens.

Day 36 of Captivity

4/20/20

There's an active conspiracy that labels everybody who disagrees with the anointed sayers of truth and variations thereof as conspiracy nuts.

Sometimes you feel like a nut. Sometimes you don't.

And that's the first thing on my list of COVID-19 pet peeves:

Pet Peeve No. 1

Just because I don't agree with you and don't blindly believe everything we're told does not make me a conspiracy nut. Conversely, if you're swallowing all the official dictums hook, line and sinker, and fighting with people who don't because they're hopeless dolts who can never be fixed but you keep trying to fix even though it's impossible, you may want to check yourself out, or in, dudes and dudettes. I believe psychologists call that projecting, or as the great philosopher, Pee-wee Herman, once put it, "I know you are, but what am I?"

Pet Peeve No. 2

Body counts are a waste of time, except to scare the bejesus out of us and keep us in line. Since they're not autopsying a majority of deaths attributed to COVID-19, there's no way of knowing if the virus contributed to any given death. There's a difference between dying with the virus and dying from the virus. That's not to say that many people aren't dying from the coronavirus, but we're being misled ... for our own good. Gee, did I forget to say thank you? *I thought by now you'd realize, there ain't no way to hide your lyin' eyes.*

Pet Peeve No. 3

And another thing, all the experts agree that we don't have a clue how many people are infected with COVID-19, and that the number is much greater than what's being reported. So why, oh why, do we keep getting ratios of deaths to exposures? Could it be to keep us lemmings in line (as long as we keep six feet behind the lemming in front of us, and six in front of the lemming behind us). A popular supposition says that if you treat people honestly, like adults, they tend to act like adults. Conversely, if you treat them like reprobates, you get *look what's happening out in the streets: Got a revolution, got to revolution!*

Pet Peeve No. 4
Preparing food. No, not eating food; I'm still real good with that. But preparing food is a never-ending pain! Going out to the diner is much easier.

Pet Peeve No. 5
Cleaning up after I eat. My wife tells me that cleaning up after myself builds character, but then on other occasions she says I'm a real character (and not in a nice way). I wish she'd make up her mind. Going out to the diner is much easier.

Pet Peeve No. 6
Talking to my wife. How much more could we possibly have to say to each other? Going out to the diner is much easier.

Day 37 of Captivity

4/21/20

Farewell spotted lanternfly, we hardly knew ye.

Before China gave us COVID-19, they gave us the spotted lanternfly, the latest-with-the-greatest scourge at the time, about to wipe out civilization as we know it.

According to the Pennsylvania Department of Agriculture's website, the spotted lanternfly is an invasive planthopper, first discovered in Berks County, and spread to other counties in the southeast portion of the state. This insect has the potential to greatly disturb agricultural crops such as grapes, hops and hardwoods. It also is reducing the quality of life for people living in heavily infested areas.

OMG! Not our quality of life!

The site goes on to say: If you see a spotted lanternfly, it's imperative to immediately report it, especially if you are not inside the quarantine zone. Kill it! Squash it! Smash it! Get rid of it, hell for leather! In the fall, these bugs will lay egg masses with 30 to 50 eggs each. These are called bad bugs for a reason; don't let them take over your county next.

Bad bugs, indeed!

Last summer, every trail, waterway landing, campsite and outdoor sporting area in this part of the state had posters warning of the potential catastrophic devastation caused by these insatiable invaders from the East. And worse, if not stopped, they could spread throughout the rest of the state and, eventually, the entire country.

The horror! The horror!

It was so frightening that we organized spotted lanternfly neighborhood watches, armed with fly swatters and flashlights (so the little buggers couldn't hide from us at night). Every day we would meet at the local mailbox kiosks in our section of the development and strategize. The strategy was always pretty much the same: Kill 'em all! Let God sort 'em out!

So, what you had was a bunch of retired folks running up and down the street, closely examining trees and shrubs, swatting like a bunch of tee-ballers swinging away at the unwelcome quality-of-life munchers.

Truthfully, I thought they were kind of beautiful and felt sorry for them, just like I do the mice in our garage that I assure my wife I'm exterminating while secretly putting cheese out for the little Mickeys. (What is it with women and mice?)

If only the misunderstood spotted lanternflies didn't attack our most precious resources: grapes and hops. We're talking wine and beer here, man. Mess with our neuroleptics and you're dead. Period. No debate. No questions asked. Beautiful or not!

But that's yesterday's news. Goodbye multitudinous spotted lanternfly, hello insidious coronavirus. Knocked you right off the front page, clear out of the paper.

It wasn't much of a contest.

But I look forward to your return to prominence and watching a bunch of old people running around fighting an enemy they have a better chance against.

Day 38 of Captivity

4/22/20

After more than five arduous weeks of preparing our own meals, my wife and I decided to order out.

We're told that we should order out to support local restaurants, that it stimulates the economy, that it's the right thing to do, that it's our civic duty, that you are what you eat so don't be fast, cheap or easy, that you should rotate your tires...

But in truth, we just didn't want to cook (ever again!).

So, I called one of our favorite bistros that we frequent regularly, one that has great wings. I was looking forward to some hot, hot, hot remembrances of days gone by.

I tried calling for more than a half hour before I got through. When I finally did, I was told, rather curtly, that it would be at least an hour and a half for delivery.

"An hour and a half!" I protested, vociferously.

"That's right, buddy."

"But I've been trying to call you for over half an hour! Are you telling me I have to invest over two hours to get your overpriced, overrated wings, you freakin' poultry pusher, you ignorant ..."

For some inexplicable reason, the guy hung up. Boy, he sure doesn't belong in the service business.

Next, I called one of our favorite Italian restaurants, a quaint little hideaway with an old-world ambiance. Before I called, my wife and I perused its menu online and had chosen the dishes we wanted. Alas, neither were available.

"It's a limited menu because of the virus," the woman on the phone told me.

Freakin' virus!

"Well, what's available?" I asked, calmly.

She started to list a few things, but when I heard ravioli, I stopped her.

"Let me look that one up," I said.

To my astonishment, the ravioli was $29.

"Twenty-nine dollars!" I elocuted emphatically. "I paid $15 last time

I had ravioli at your place, you freakin' price-gougers, you freakin' opportunistic chiselers. I wouldn't eat your crappy food if you paid me, you freakin' …"

Another hang-up. Geez, the stress from this isolation is really getting to people.

When I told my wife what had happened, she looked at me like I was something stuck to the bottom of her shoe (not a look I'm not used to). "You were looking at the lobster ravioli," she said with undisguised disgust.

"Oh," was all I could manage.

Finally, I called a nearby national chain famous for hamburgers, but neither of us wanted a burger so we ordered a soup and sandwich combo. After I placed the order, the young woman asked me to hold. When she came back a few minutes later, she said, "We don't make soup."

"You don't make soup?" I asked, graciously. "You're not making soup tonight?"

"We don't make soup."

"But it's online in your temporary menu," I said, less graciously.

"We don't make soup."

"Then why is it on your menu?" I asked, not so graciously.

"We don't make soup."

"I know, you don't make soup. I get it. But why's it on the menu?" I persisted as graciously left town on the last train.

"We don't make soup."

"What is this, a Monty Python routine?"

"We don't make soup."

My wife picked up the order and we sat down to a relaxed and hassle-free meal. Unfortunately, the sandwiches were poorly constructed with hard-to-locate portions of bacon and avocado, the big sellers for the item, which effectively buzzkilled the relaxing interlude. Then my wife dropped a bomb on me: She told me they had put a 20 percent gratuity on the bill.

"For what? Did you pay it?" I asked, becoming less and less hassle-free.

"Yes. What else could I have done?" she asked.

"What else could you have done," I responded in a non-relaxed fashion.

I immediately picked up my phone and called the restaurant. When I got the manager, I expressed my dismay: "There was a 20 percent gratuity on our bill. Was that a mistake?"

"Oh, no," he said, all jolly like he was delivering the best news ever. "We believe our employees, who are working through this difficult time, deserve it. We feel it's the right thing to do."

"Isn't that supposed to be the customer's decision?" I asked, agitation rising.

"This way it's easier for our customers. We're always putting our customers first."

"Look, fool," I seethed. "Take that 20 percent off our bill immediately because I wouldn't tip anybody on your staff 10 cents for delivering a bag of sandwiches that looked like they were made by a monkey, you freakin' moron, you pointy-headed piece of …"

Click!

Man, with all the polarization out there, it's really hard to have a decent conversation with anybody.

Day 39 of Captivity

4/23/20

Today, I was going to write about my father, but decided not to. I was going to tell you that he died from the virus, at least that's what it says on his death certificate.

They didn't perform an autopsy, so we can never be certain if that was the actual cause of his death. He had underlying conditions: He drank too much and he had some problems with his heart, so who knows? He lived alone (a red flag for older men).

I was going to tell you that this was in 1978, 42 years ago when he was only 53 and we took the flu for granted. I wanted to tell you that the flu kills more than 56,000 people every year in the United States — 80,000 in 2017. My father caught the flu from somebody else, probably an ordinary guy going about his business who might not have even known he had it. That type of behavior wasn't considered criminal in those days; that was just life.

And death.

Before I decided not to write this, I wanted to tell you that life is dangerous; people die, that it's always tragic when it's somebody close to you, especially when it's from something as seemingly innocuous as the flu. I know. So please save your lectures about the ravishes of virus-related death and your preaching on the irresponsible behavior of people living their lives. Here's a clue: Empathy is not sublimation for a feeling of inadequacy manifested in overt displays of disingenuous and boastful declaration of concern for others.

In other words, it's not about what a grand person you are.

I didn't want to bore you today by writing about a new report just published in the Journal of the American Medical Association stating, "Researchers found that fever wasn't a reliable warning sign of [COVID-19] infection. Just one-third of patients had elevated temperatures when they were triaged upon arrival (at the hospital)."

Remember way back to yesterday when a fever was the telltale sign of coronavirus? That means two-thirds (or most) of the infected people this study examined DIDN'T have a fever.

Helter skelter, helter skelter, helter skelter!

Here's some advice I was going to give you about symptoms of COVID-19: If you feel sick, call your doctor or go to the emergency room. If you don't feel sick, then go on with your … oh wait, I forgot. You're not allowed to go on with your life.

When logic and proportion have fallen sloppy dead.

Another curious episode in my life I wanted to tell you about but wasn't sure you'd want to hear happened the other day while I was on a bike ride. I was on a paved trail crowded with other cyclists and walkers. A bug must have gotten under my sunglasses and lodged in my eye, so I stopped, took off my helmet and sunglasses, leaned my head way back and tried to get the bug out. After a few minutes, a couple walking by stopped and looked up at the sky. They must have thought I saw something way up yonder. Soon, another person stopped and looked up, then a bicyclist stopped, straddled her bike and looked up, too. Pretty soon I had a gaggle of people standing around me, looking up at the sky.

Finally, somebody asked, "What are we looking at?"

Somebody else responded, "It's hard to see."

"What is it?" somebody else asked.

"It's difficult to make out," another offered.

"Oh, I think I see it," from another person.

"Where is it?" someone asked.

"Over there," somebody said, and soon everybody was pointing to the sky.

"Oh, yeah," someone shouted. "I think I see it."

"There is it," someone else chimed in, and pretty soon they were all a-buzz over nothing in the sky.

"Curiouser and curiouser!" cried Alice.

No, I didn't want to write about any of that stuff; I wanted to write about the weather.

It really sucks, right?

4/26/20

Please allow me to take this opportunity to thank you for your thoughtful notes of gratitude and encouragement over my COVID-19 provocative essays.

I hope they're bringing you a little respite from the stress of our "new normal." To show my appreciation for your kindness, I'm going to answer a few questions.

Question No. 1: Do you take the coronavirus seriously?
Answer No. 1: I take the seriously ill and the seriously dead very seriously. I take the moderately ill and moderately dead moderately seriously. I take the politicians and the media not seriously at all. In this time of inflated numbers, inflated exposers and inflated egos, it's hard to figure out the difference between valid, helpful information and expedience, like trying to separate the pepper from the fly shit.

Question No. 2: Are you afraid of catching the virus?
Answer No. 2: I don't want to catch the virus, but I'm not afraid of catching the virus. In the long run, fear will do more damage than pestilence. Perhaps I have a false sense of safety because I've never had the flu of any kind, and I think I may have some sort of immunity. Also, my blood type is O negative. There's a theory out there that people with type O blood are invulnerable to the disease, so for all of you with non-type O blood:

> *I'll be seeing you*
> *In all the old familiar places*
> *That this heart of mine*
> *Embraces all day and through.*

Question No. 3: Are you looking forward to getting a haircut?
Answer No. 3: No, not if I have to wear a mask. I don't know how you can cut someone's hair who's wearing a mask tied around his head or looped over her ears. It's like trying to fry a chicken with the feathers still on. (That's terrible, I know, but I couldn't think of a clever metaphor. Let me try again.) It's like trying to cut the grass with lot of

stuff in the way. (That's just plain stupid!) It's like trying to scramble an egg without breaking the shell. (They're getting worse.) Okay, it's like trying to _____ with _____ (fill in the blanks, Einstein). I just know there are going to be a lot of wrecked face masks, and a lot of bad hairdos. I think I'll grow a ponytail.

Question No. 4: Are you going to inject yourself with bleach?
Answer No. 4: There you go again! Everybody's always misinterpreting President Trump. He wasn't talking about ingesting bleach; he was talking about what he uses on his hair.

Question No. 5: Are you going to publish these pieces in a book?
Answer No. 5: Only if all of you buy my new book right away, so run to your cellphones or computers immediately (oh, you're already there?) and bring up *www.howtoselltheplague.com*. It's already marked down to half price in an effort to help fight the plague. And remember, no sharing. If I catch you, I'm going to report you to local authorities for not maintaining proper social distancing.

Question No. 6: You don't like Governor Wolf, do you?
Answer No. 6: With him in charge, it feels like we're always on double-secret probation; like we're being lectured that fat, drunk and stupid is no way to go through life. Ha! Look around you at the capitol building, Guv.

Question No. 7: Do you have any good news for us?
Answer No. 7: I do, some really good news. Apparently, COVID-19 has pretty much wiped out almost every heretofore known deadly force. Nobody is any longer dying from heart or lung diseases, cancers, high blood pressure, diabetes, car accidents, electrocution, falls at home, ingrown toenails, etc. The way it looks, once we beat this thing, nobody will ever die again.

Ain't that good news? Man ain't that news?

Day 43 of Captivity

It's a dog's life.
Especially now.
But not so much for cats.

Really, cats couldn't care less. As a matter of fact, cats prefer owners to show up twice a day to feed them and then be gone. Sometimes they appreciate a warm body to snuggle up to, but they also enjoy lying in the sun. Same thing.

What? You thought it was you they liked? In truth (and you know it), cats aren't capable of making commitments. (What does that tell you about you, all you cat-picture sharers?)

Not dogs. They are the commitment champions of the world with no time for losers (of the feline variety) 'cause they are the slobber-all-over-you champions of the world. And then along comes the coronavirus with its house arrest (that I hear Governor Wolf's going to double down on by issuing ankle bracelets to all those people the snitch police catch thinking for themselves), and dogs (not cats, regardless of how much you fool yourself) throughout the land who delight in spending more quality time with their masters. For some, that means lying on the couch with your master 18 hours a day watching television instead of the usual four hours. For others, it means doing a lot more stuff together all day long, whether or not your master wants you following his every step and sometimes in-between his steps from sunup to sundown.

My dog's sure happy about the situation. You can tell because she's always smiling. I know, they say dogs can't smile, but they also tell you dogs are color-blind. And just how do they know that? I bet it's the same scientist who told us COVID-19 can't be spread person-to-person. Of course dogs can see color; they certainly can see the difference between green grass and brown poop — have you ever seen a dog eat grass?

Callie, my dog, likes to lie by my feet in the morning in my office as I write these provocative essays. She's my first reader, although she can't really read. I have to read them to her, and if she likes the piece, she just lies there. If she doesn't like the piece, she just lies there. If she just lies there, I assume she likes it. She's my favorite critic.

Callie likes joining me for my midmorning nap. And my midafternoon nap. And my early evening nap. She needs those naps, though. With me home all day, she's not getting her requisite 20 hours a day of sleep. She's rather ambivalent concerning the new normal, sleep-wise.

But eating makes up for any loss of her slumberland sojourns. She usually eats twice a day, but with me home and suffering from Coronavirus Gluttony Disorder (CGD: a side effect of not having COVID-19, or maybe a side effect of having COVID-19 — who knows, since more and more scientists are telling us that two plus two equals 52,384 ... I mean, are they now telling us that most people with COVID-19 don't even know they have it?) and displaying the classic symptoms (eating six meals a day plus snacks), she's quite busy.

You know the best part of having a dog for a guy? Not having to clean up all the food we drop on the floor. Given the extraordinary circumstances wherein we find ourselves, it's a veritable nonstop smorgasbord for Callie.

I keep telling her she better watch her weight, and she just lies there ... obviously agreeing with me.

4/28/20

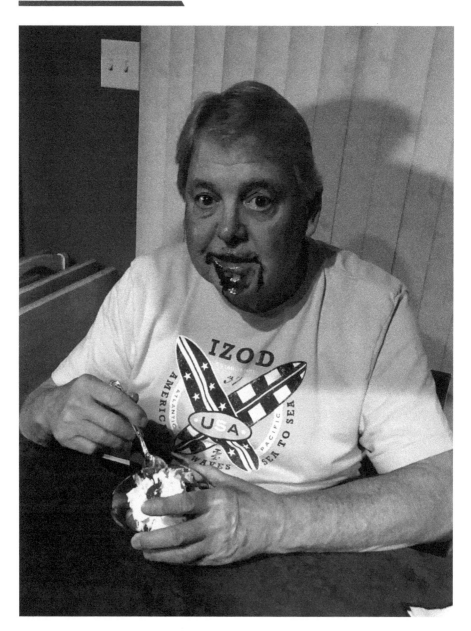

Everybody's talking at me. I don't hear a word they're saying.

The Black Death, more commonly known as The Plague, was a bubonic pestilence that struck Europe in the mid-14th century. It's hard to get accurate counts on its devastation because the numbers have been so grossly exaggerated (imagine that!), but best-guess estimates are that more than 20 million people perished, wiping out at least a third of the continent's population.

In other words, it was the real deal.

That was 700 years ago, and in that time (according to reliable sources), fewer words have been used to discuss it than have been written, spoken and/or idiotized in the past two months regarding our current minor pandemic. *Whatayatalk, whatayatalk, whatayatalk, whatayatalk, whatayatalk?*

With the proliferous pontification belligerently bombarding us in a bountiful bouquet of bullshit, it's hard to see the difference between the bombastic and the buffoonery. They say that the first casualty of war is truth, and make no mistake about it, we are at war. And worse, we have to fight this damn pandemic at the same time.

So, let us, you and I, take a look at some of the casualties of this war we were drafted into.

Truth: Remember playing whisper down the lane in elementary school when a message was whispered from one person to another, and by the time it got to the end of the line it was a different message? Guess what? Those messages were more accurate than the stuff we're getting in the news. That's right, folks, elementary school kids are more trustworthy than our politicians and the media in interpreting information. Truth, justice and the American way are up, up and away, replaced by an insatiable gluttony for ratings and votes.

Compassion: It always bothers me when I hear people say that 58,000 Americans were killed in Vietnam, as if 58,000 is a single thing. Numbers are dehumanizing, and it's difficult to grasp the true nature of loss when a person is reduced to a number. In reality, there are

57,939 names on the Vietnam Veterans Memorial wall in Washington D.C., and four of those names belong to guys I knew in high school. The first time I visited the wall and saw those names, it completely changed my perspective on the Vietnam War. Having not been there, it was just a concept to me, but the wall changed all that. I feel the same way when I see the COVID-19 body counts ticking off on the news networks. Each one of those ticks is a person with a life left behind, and not simply a prop for dramatic effect. It makes me sick.

Economy: It feels like we've used a hydrogen bomb to destroy an anthill. Most of the models were wrong, and there's no empirical evidence that any of the sacrifices we've made have had any appreciable effect on the virus, only supposition. Conversely, the herd immunization theory used in other places seems to have yielded the same results as ours. At this point, the best scientific thinking seems to be: Who knows? The bottom line is that there will be no bottom line if we keep this up much longer. The economy is already on life support — many small businesses won't make it, and many large businesses will suck off all the nectar to stay afloat. As bad as it's been, the worst is yet to come. Fortunately, our leaders have not been drastically affected and are financially okay. Thank God, right?

Health: Okay, okay, okay! We're eating like pigs, and really, really bad stuff, at that. And yeah, we're not going to the gym or working out much, but so what. As Country Joe and the Fish so aptly put it: "Well, there ain't no time to wonder why, whoopee! We're all gonna die." Please pass the whipped cream.

Day 45 of Captivity

4/29/20

During his daily press briefing, Governor Tom Wolf of Pennsylvania announces plans to ease some of the restrictions on residents of the state. Let's listen in.

Governor Wolf: We have opened up all state-run liquor stores in the commonwealth for curbside pickup.

Reporter: People have had problems getting through to the few stores you had previously opened. We've been told that was because there was only one phone line going into each store. What have you done to correct that situation?

Governor Wolf: That's not true! That's not true! Let's try to get this right. We had only one phone line for all the stores. In these troubling times, we need to be fiscally responsible, not fiscally irresponsible, and wasting money on a line for each store would not be fiscally responsible and would be fiscally irresponsible.

Reporter: But Your Holiness, you've allowed the stores to be open for extremely limited hours and people can't get through to place orders.

Governor Wolf: In these troubling times, we all must act responsibly, not irresponsibly. The great citizens of the great commonwealth of Pennsylvania have always answered the bell and acted responsibly, not irresponsibly.

Reporter: That answer doesn't make any sense.

Governor Wolf: Who's on first?

Reporter: What?

Governor Wolf: What's on second.

Reporter: I don't know.

Governor Wolf: Third base.

Reporter: What other measures are you taking, Master Tom?

Governor Wolf: We're opening up the ski areas. Balancing the needs for physical and mental health with the ongoing fight against a deadly virus is our goal. Skiing accomplishes all those things.

Reporter: How does skiing help fight the virus, Lord Tom?

Governor Wolf: I've consulted with the best scientific minds on this subject and I'm told that skiers go fast, too fast for the virus to catch them, so the more people we have going fast, the less chance the virus has of catching them. We are encouraging slow skiers to go fishing instead. The Game Commission could use the revenue, which is a perfectly valid reason to allow trout season to open.

Reporter: But Big Cheese, there's no snow.

Governor Wolf: More cowbell!

Reporter: What's the status of unemployment benefits for self-employed Pennsylvanians, Duke, Duke, Duke of Earl(ly onset senility)?

Governor Wolf: We are working on that, but I won't be able to disclose where we are in that process at this time. However, I will at a later date to be named at a later date during a press conference at a later date.

Reporter: People are complaining that they can't get through to the unemployment office on the phone.

Governor Wolf: We already covered that — the phone line thing.

Reporter: You mean you have only one phone line coming into the state capital for all government business?

Governor Wolf: Oh no, we have several lines, but only one is working right now. Most of the lines come into my office, but we've had to shut them down — and it has nothing to do with me not wanting to talk to my subjects, either. I've consulted with the best scientific minds on this subject, and I'm told that they're not sure, but they suspect that the coronavirus germs can travel through phone lines, especially those phone lines coming into my office. It's an enigma, but we're working on it, and I'll get back to you on that later at a later date to be named at a later date in the future.

Reporter: That doesn't sound right — Hail, Caesar!

Governor Wolf: Sometimes they get it wrong. And if being wrong is right, then I don't want to be wrong ... or right.

Reporter: I wouldn't worry too much about that, Your Highness.

Governor Wolf: More good news: We're opening up beach volleyball.

Reporter: Excuse me, Meine Führer, but there are no beaches in Pennsylvania.

Governor Wolf: Are too! We have lovely beaches in Erie.

Reporter: Have you ever been to Erie?

Governor Wolf: Don't be silly. Nobody goes to Erie.

Reporter: Is that going to be open for both men and women?

Governor Wolf: No, just for women. I've consulted with the best scientific minds on this subject and I'm told that men present a greater danger of being exposed to the virus because they have more skin.

Reporter: Does this decision have anything to do with itsy-bitsy, teeny-weeny bikinis, Your Royal Heinie?

Governor Wolf: Sometimes they get it right.

Day 46 of Captivity

4/30/20

Neil Armstrong said, "People love conspiracy theories."

For those of you who went to high school to study how to take standardized tests instead of, you know, learning stuff, Armstrong used to be the first man to walk on the moon, but is now the first person to walk on the moon, and he famously said, "That's one small step for man, one giant leap for mankind" (which soon will be edited so as not to offend anybody, if that's even possible).

The man knew all about conspiracy theories, too, because there are people who seriously believe we never went to the moon, that it was staged in the desert of New Mexico. I wrote about that in my book *Dancing in the Cave of the Dragon*:

"In its July 2-9, 2018 issue, Sports Illustrated dubbed Lonnie Walker IV (a professional basketball player from nearby Reading) the most interesting rookie in the world.

"And that's very interesting.

"Because one of the questions SI asked him was whether he believes (in) the moon landings. He answered, 'The background, the surroundings — y'all tried to make it look too much like a moon. The details were almost too great. There's no way it looks this nice or this well done.

"So, if I understand Professor Walker correctly, the moon landings were fake because the moon didn't look fake enough?

"Now that's interesting."

I never believed that particular conspiracy theory, and I don't believe that the United States government blew up the World Trade Center, or that Proctor & Gamble is part of the occult (but I have serious doubts about Nabisco because those Oreo cookies must be the devil's doing), or any other wacked-out, paranoid ravings. But there is one conspiracy I do believe: President Kennedy was not killed by Lee Harvey Oswald. As a matter of fact, Oswald had nothing to do with the assassination. I've spent the past 57 years studying the horrific events in Dallas on November 22, 1963, and I'm confident I could put doubts in your mind if you were to, say, buy me a few beers one evening after this gilded cage is finally opened.

And when I awoke I was alone. This bird had flown.

Conspiracies are a funny business. In today's over-communicated world, everything's a conspiracy, everybody's out to get us. That's because we've been taught that nothing's our fault. Personal responsibility? Are you kidding? That bird flew the cage a long time ago.

Conspiracies galore! And the best part about a conspiracy is that most of the participants don't even know they're part of a conspiracy.

Cool, huh?

It's fun to watch the current COVID-19 version of conspirators fighting against the other guy's conspiracy. And those fighters for truth and justice are pretty flexible. If their handlers point right, they run like crazy to the right; if the handlers point left, off they go a scurrying to the left. It's like watching a cross between Simon Says and The Hokey Pokey.

Reminds me of an episode of the *Rockford Files*. In "The Farnsworth Stratagem," Jim Rockford cons a group of underworld figures by convincing them there's oil or gas under their condominiums. He sets up a big oil rig in the front court and goes through the whole charade of drilling. When they finally hit the water main to the building and water gushes out of the derrick, Angel Martin, Rockford's ne'er-do-well sidekick, starts running all over the place screaming, "Oil! Oil! Oil." Jim grabs him and tells him it's gas, and Angel proceeds to keep running hither and yon, yelling like a madman, "Gas! Gas! Gas!"

With all the malleable facts swirling around the coronavirus, it's hard for the objectified co-conspirators to keep track of whether it's oil or gas.

But take heart, all ye cabal devotees; there definitely is a major conspiracy enveloping you. As John Updike put it; "America is a vast conspiracy ... to make you happy."

In every life we have some trouble. When you worry you make it double. Don't worry, be happy.

5/3/20

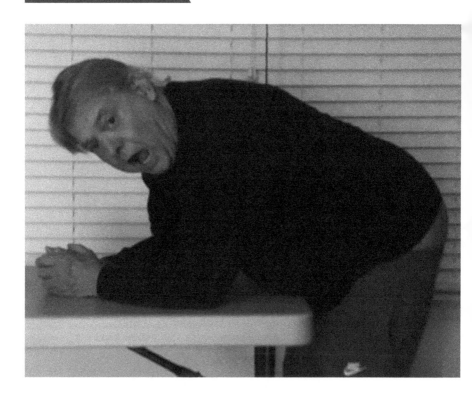

I was running errands this weekend when I ran into my friend Bob.

We stood the requisite six feet apart and muffled through our face masks about the coronavirus. (What else do people muffle about these days?) Bob told me an interesting story concerning a doctor visit that I thought I'd share with you.

As the pollen increased during the spring, Bob's allergies kicked up like they do every year, so he called his doctor, Dr. Botch A. Lism, to get a prescription for an antihistamine. Dr. Lism's nurse triaged Bob over the phone.

Nurse: What seems to be the problem, Bob?

Bob: I'm having my usual allergy problems and I need a prescription.

Nurse: Please describe your symptoms, Bob.

Bob: Runny nose, itchy eyes, sore throat, cough, congestion, all the regular stuff.

Nurse: Oh my, Bob. Please hold while I confer with the doctor.

Finally, the nurse came back.

Nurse: The doctor wants to see you immediately, Bob. Can you come in this afternoon?

Bob: Sure, but what's the problem?

Nurse: During this virus epidemic, we have to take extra precautions. It's the new normal, Bob.

Upon arrival, Bob was ushered into the doctor's examination room.

Dr. Lism: Please describe your symptoms.

Bob: Like I told your nurse, Doc, I have a runny nose, itchy eyes, sore throat, cough, congestion, all the signs of my allergies.

Dr. Lism: Hmm, I see. How's your appetite?

Bob: I always lose my appetite; you know that. I get that postnasal drip thing and it makes me sick to my stomach.

Dr. Lism: You have an upset stomach?

Bob: Well, yeah.

Dr. Lism shook his head.

Dr. Lism: Any aches in your joints?

Bob: Oh sure, but you know I need knee replacements.

Dr. Lism: Uh huh. What about your … bowel movements? How are your … bowel movements?

Bob: My … bowel movements are moving along just fine.

Dr. Lism: Oh, that's not good.

Bob: What's going on here, Doc? What's the problem?

Dr. Lism placed the palm of his hand on Bob's chest and pushed.

Dr. Lism: Do you have any chest pain?

Bob: Yeah! That hurts like hell.

Dr. Lism: I'm afraid I have some bad news for you, Bob. I believe you've been infected with COVID-19. You have all the classic symptoms: runny nose, itchy eyes, sore throat, cough, congestion, achy joints, stomachache, chest pain, diarrhea, night sweats and a low-grade fever. You fit the bill perfectly, I'm sorry to say.

Bob thought it odd that Dr. Lism was smiling.

Bob: But I don't have diarrhea. My stools are fine.

Dr. Lism scribbled some notes.

Dr. Lism: That's not good, hard stools.

Bob: But you just said diarrhea was a sign of the virus?

Dr. Lism: Diarrhea or hard stools; both very, very bad.

Bob: And I don't have night sweats. Where'd you get that?

Dr. Lism: I can tell from looking at you, Bob. I am a trained medical expert, you know.

Bob: But you didn't take my temperature. How do you know I have a fever?

Dr. Lism picked up the phone.

Dr. Lism: Nurse, please come in here.

Nurse: Yes, doctor?

Dr. Lism: Please take Bob's temperature.

The nurse placed her hand on Bob's forehead.

Nurse: 101.4.

Dr. Lism: Thank you, nurse. Please call the county and tell them we have another COVID-19 diagnosis.

Bob could hear the nurse on the phone.

Nurse: We've got another one for you.

Bob heard the clang of a bell.

Bob: Shouldn't I get tested?

Dr. Lism: Tests? We don't need no stinking tests!

Bob: Doctor, are you sure about this?

Dr. Lism put his finger on Bob's wrist.

Dr. Lism: Just as I suspected.

Bob: What is it, Doc?

Dr. Lism: You have a pulse.

Bob: Is that bad?

Dr. Lism: A pulse is the surest way to tell if someone has the virus. It's the latest symptom issued by the CDC.

Bob sat there in silence for a few seconds, letting it sink in.

Dr. Lism: Please drop your pants and bend over.

Bob: Do I need a proctology exam, Doc?

Dr. Lism: It's a new directive from Governor Wolf. He wants us to prepare people for what they'll be getting when the bill for all this comes due.

Bob: Ouch! That really smarts!

Dr. Lism: Don't worry, Governor Wolf won't feel a thing.

Bob: What now, Doc? Should I quarantine myself?

Dr. Lism: That's not a bad idea. Get rest and drink lots of liquids. Call us immediately if you get worse and we'll rush you to the hospital. It's hard to count … you know, when someone's … you know, at home.

Bob: You think I'm going to die?!

Dr. Lism: Of course not … but keep a good thought.

5/4/20

President Trump and his coronavirus task force held a press briefing yesterday, and I was lucky enough to get a transcript of the covfefe.

President Trump: I have some really tremendous news; really, really tremendous news: We're winning! Really, we've won! Everything will be back up and running next week. Make America the old normal again!

Dr. Fauci: Mr. President, you can't say that! We haven't gotten in front of this thing yet. We're still far away from opening up the economy, regardless of how many people's lives it destroys when it comes to saving .03 percent of our country from the devastating COVID-19. We don't even know the depth of this crisis yet; we're still calculating its life span. So far, we're up to the 13th wave projected to hit in March 2025 — unless we can develop a vaccine — but since FDA approval will take about 10 years, we're not out of the woods yet. The stage we're at now is that we're looking for our car in the parking lot.

President Trump: I was being sarcastic — very sarcastic — just to see what would happen. You people, believe me, you people can't keep up with me. I'm a very sarcastic guy. I'm an incredibly sarcastic guy.

New York City Mayor Bill de Blasio muscles his way to the podium.

Mayor de Blasio: The coronavirus is all Donald Trump's fault. He's killing Americans! Everything is Trump's fault!

President Trump: That's fake news! When this virus broke, Billy Boy, weren't you the one who told New Yorkers to go out to dinner and a show?

Mayor de Blasio: I was being sarcastic — very sarcastic — just to see what would happen. I'm a very sarcastic guy.
The mayor is being dragged from the stage.

President Trump: I want to announce that Mayor de Blasio, in a really, really wonderful gesture, a great gesture, has volunteered to try a Lysol injection.

Mayor de Blasio: Did not!

President Trump: Did too, you loser. What a moron.

Mayor de Blasio: Am not!

Dr. Birx walks up to the podium.

Dr. Birx: We're not calculating our death counts the same way Europe is. In Europe, they're not counting dead cats and dogs …

Nancy Pelosi pushes aside Dr. Birx.

Speaker Pelosi: Joe Biden knows how to get the job done. I'm proud to endorse him …

Nancy Pelosi is edged off the podium by the President.

President Trump: Where'd you park your broom, Nancy?

Speaker Pelosi: Blow it out your ear, you orange buffoon!

President Trump: Have some ice cream, Nancy.

Speaker Pelosi: Blow it out your blowhole, you orange buffoon!

President Trump: Incidentally, Speaker Pelosi has agreed to join Mayor de Blasio in the Lysol challenge.

Speaker Pelosi: Did not!

Pennsylvania Governor Tom Wolf rushes up to the dais.

Governor Wolf: Everything I've done has been perfect!

President Trump: Hey stupid, that's my line.

Nancy Pelosi charges back to the podium.

Speaker Pelosi: Joe Biden is Joe Biden!

President Clinton: That depends on what the meaning of "is" is.

Surgeon General Jerome Adams takes the podium.

Vice Admiral Adams: You should be wearing masks because wearing a mask could help slow down the spread of the virus. On the other hand, wearing a mask could help spread the virus even faster. So, ladies and gentlemen, take my advice, pull down your pants and slide on the ice.

Steven Wright: On the other hand, you have different fingers.

President Trump: This is going to be huge. This is going to be historic; really, really historic … huge … and historic. It's going to be hugely historic. We're going to make America great again and restore everybody's constitutional rights.

Joe Biden stumbles onto the stage.

Joe Biden: No ordinary American cares about his constitutional rights.

President Trump: Who woke up Uncle Joe?

Joe Biden: Is it lunch yet?

Speaker Pelosi: We love Joe!

President Trump: Your coven's calling, Nancy. They need your help with the brew.

Speaker Pelosi: Double bubble, toil and trouble. Blow real hard and bubbles double.

President Trump: Thank all of you for your tremendous, really tremendous dedication to our great, great nation. This is huge, this is the greatest group, the most incredible group ever assembled in our fantastic country's history to fight COVID-19. Everything we're doing is beautiful, it's all beautiful, very, very beautiful, and the beauty of me is that I'm very rich. And smart. Very rich and very smart. We're all in this together, me being very rich and very smart, and you guys.

5/5/20

I hope the force was with you yesterday and the real Corona is with you today.

And while we're in a celebratory mood, let us mark our 50th day of captivity with a celebration of the COVID-19 good times.

Come on and let the good times roll. We're gonna stay here till we soothe our souls.

One of my biggest bugaboos in this glorious entanglement is my hair — I can't get it cut. Unlike Chicago Mayor Lori Lightfoot, I'm not a public figure, I'm not on national media and I'm not out in the public eye (unless the public eye goes to Wegmans or my local beer store). That's the rationale she used to go to her hair stylist (stylist being a relative term), while the rest of Chicago remained in lockdown where they're *hairy noon and night, hair that's a fright. [They're] hairy high and low, don't ask [them] why — don't know!*

I guess that's the same excuse other public figures out in the public eye are using to separate themselves from the rest of us who are not all together in this together. Maybe that's been the plan all along, to make it easier for the privileged elite to spot we many, we dreadlocked many, and separate themselves from the *bangled, tangled, spangled* masses they so desperately need for support … from as far away as possible.

We all need to pull together, right!

My hair's a mess and could really use a trim. I usually get it cut every three to four weeks, and my last was in early March. That means I'm into my third cycle without a touch-up, which puts me in that in-between stage of sloppy-sloth and old-man-trying-to-look-hip.

The good news is I'm saving money. My haircuts cost $25, including tip, so I've got an extra 75 bucks in my pocket by now. Since nobody knows how long we'll be held prisoner to Gov. Wolf's clandestine formula for devaluing Pennsylvanian businesses, I could end up with a three-figure bonanza, probably enough to buy a car dealership by the time this is over.

Murder hornets, right?

I bought my first tank of gas in a long time yesterday. I think I'm getting about 30 days to the gallon (okay, I stole that — so what else is new?) — and I paid less than $2 a gallon. Cheap gas and nowhere to go! Not only is that a bummer for us road warriors, but the state is losing a bundle. The Tom Wolf gas tax of 58.7 cents per gallon is the highest in the land. Wow! A guy who can't seem to find his ass with a flashlight sure knows how to get into your pocket.

Master of the house. Keeper of the zoo. Ready to relieve 'em of a sou or two.

And how about that new "care" emoji on Facebook — another superficial way to express our pretend true feelings. Kudos to the gang over there in cyber never-never land and their ageless prankster leader, Zuck Pan. They care so much about us and our well-being that they're making sure we don't have to read anything that might confuse us or make us think. From now on, they'll do all of our thinking for us. Along with their pals at Google/YouTube, we are finally liberated from the mundane task of developing opinions.

Trust the experts, right!

There was a young man named Zuck
Who insisted that he didn't suck.
He built a platform to ensure all conform,
But he was a real useless _____.*

*Guess the magic word and win a chance to buy my new book.

5/6/20

Boy, do we bend language to fit our needs.

Like "unprecedented times" quickly rivaling "draconian" as the best use of verbiage for the dim and the dull — terrific subterfuge to mask a lack of original thought and an underlining yet pervasive vapidity. If I hear that threadbare epithet from one more lacquered, two-dimensional news drone, I'm going to go all draconian and create some very real and unpleasant unprecedented times.

Look, all times are unprecedented simply because they've never happened before. The word means new and original, and every day is new and original. Maybe not as exciting and expedient as the coronavirus, but every day is one of a kind. Simply saying these "challenging times" or these "difficult days" isn't profound-sounding enough — they just don't feed the murder hornets — and in no way do they conjure up the essential images of doom and gloom to send the shuddering herd into a debilitating spasm of fear and loathing.

Unprecedented times! OMG! The end is near!

No, I don't believe "draconian" and "unprecedented times" are appropriate apocalyptic appellations for these draconian and unprecedented times wherein we struggle within this hall-of-mirrors reality. Instead, I prefer "hypocrisy" as our watchword.

According to Merriam-Webster, the definition of hypocrisy is "a feigning to be what one is not, or to believe what one does not: behavior that contradicts what one claims to believe or feel. The false assumption of an appearance of virtue or religion." A relatively easy word to understand, but an almost impossible concept to apply to oneself, although the false assumption of virtue is a powerful elixir against the fears and anxieties of murdering dear old grandma and grandpa by irresponsible breathing.

I've already written extensively about the duplicity of our leaders and the media (and I imagine I will continue to do so as long as this thing lasts — and when I say "this thing," I mean the human race — because the material is so bountiful and unceasing). Today, instead, I want to make it more personal, make it more about people I know who possess so little self-awareness or are so obtuse that they are definitely off my tequila-drinking buddy list (unless, of course, they're buying).

When a corps of frustrated and desperate people who were worried about making a living and feeding their families marched on Harrisburg in the grand American tradition of civil disobedience, a personage of my acquaintance, who doesn't have children, criticized the marchers on Facebook for being reckless and selfish. This person tends to place a high importance on her causes of choice, but apparently hungry and scared kids don't fit into that agenda. (Empathy is a one-way street for so many these days.) Worse, she allowed the most hateful comments on her post. One woman suggested that they all should die from the virus because one of them held a sign that read, "Give me liberty or give me death."

When I say she allowed those types of comments, that's exactly what she did. You have editorial control over your posts on Facebook, so you can delete anything you don't like or feel is inappropriate (like I do when I feel someone hasn't fully captured the essence of my true awesomeness).

Which another woman I know also failed to do, and instead chose to castigate someone for making a political comment about her thinly disguised political post. (Regrettably, all posts regarding the coronavirus contain an element of politics since we've reached the point of you're either with us or against us.) She would insist her post was apolitical because ideologues never know they're ideologues and can't see the forests through the memes and GIFs and emojis. So instead of removing the offending comment, she chose to embarrass the writer about being inappropriately political, and by doing so exposed her veiled desire to make a political statement.

Unfortunately, hypocrisy is an inevitable byproduct of a society that has turned on itself. There was great hope that the pandemic would bring us all back together, but it has only served to separate us even further. That would suggest the pandemic is less a medical issue than a political one. And, unfortunately, today's politics are all about hypocrisy.

Like the guy who reads my posts every day and then writes to me on Messenger about how insulting and sophomoric my rantings are and that I should be tarred and feathered and put in stocks and hung by my toes from the nearest tree and, in general, be treated not nice. Now there's a guy who has fully captured the essence of my true awesomeness.

5/7/20

Because I'm a big fan of retreads (especially when they litter the highway with huge chunks of rubber that can smash your windshield and make you forget all about the coronavirus), and because I have a propensity for beating horses to death (metaphorically speaking, of course — I've never actually beaten a horse in any manner, although many a nag running a length or two behind has contributed to a fairly substantial beatdown of me), let us return then, you and I, to my list of pet peeves.

Pet Peeve No.7

Cyber scissors gone wild! Seriously, this censorship business is serious. How can our political leaders, who have sworn to uphold the Constitution, allow this kind of tyranny to go on? How can a few dweebs decide what is appropriate material for American consumption? How is it legal for the Silicon Valley nerd patrol to use their social media platforms (that have practically become utilities) to censor what offends their underdeveloped, emotionally sophomoric ids, and to deny free speech because it violates some narrow, puerile vison of what the world should be? Where's the outrage? When did Americans become sheep? What ever happened to, "I disagree with what you say, but I'll defend with my life your right to say it?" Imagine if someone listened to your phone calls and bleeped out anything they didn't think was good for you. It's the same thing, only worse. With social media, they get to decide to whom you speak. This isn't about what I say today; it's about what you say tomorrow.

Pet Peeve No.8

Don't you just love those unsolicited emails soliciting you to give some stranger control over your website, your marketing plan or your money, and the sender's email comes from a Yahoo or Gmail address. Give me a break! Just because I sent that Nigerian prince five grand to help him recover his fortune that he's eventually going to split with me, it doesn't mean I'm a complete rube. Oh no you don't! I know a scam when I see one.

Pet Peeve No.9

Do you think *Saturday Night Live* will lampoon Chris Cuomo for being sick with COVID-19 every night on his CNN show and then spending weekends at his property in the Hamptons where he moves around the hood fairly freely, sans mask and with little consideration for social distancing? No, I don't think so either.

Pet Peeve No.10

Want to know how to create a meat shortage? Tell everybody there's a meat shortage.

Pet Peeve No.11

Like me, are you sick to death of all those disingenuous, touchy-feely television commercials from opportunistic companies extolling us for our great work at staying home and doing nothing while they're with us 100 percent and will be there when this is over to sell us their crappy stuff at exorbitant prices while paying their Third World workers sub-living wages as they contaminate and pollute?

Pet Peeve No.12

When the coronavirus was at its peak a few weeks ago, before they started digging up bodies from potter's field to examine them for the COVID-19 (and surprisingly, they all have it) and adding symptoms to encompass everybody with blue or brown eyes (and some *green-eyed ladies, lovely ladies,* too), we were free to go in and out of grocery or hardware stores as we pleased. Now, with things getting better, we have to stand in line to get into grocery and hardware stores — kind of like putting the cart before the horse's ass (or as we Pennsylvanians like to call it, Governor Tom Wolf). Once you get into the stores, they're practically empty and you can zip through your shopping. Meanwhile, out in front of the store at we'll-show-you-who's-boss central, the folks are schmoozing and talking and standing close together and enjoying some good old-fashioned unprotected social intercourse. News flash: Governor Wolf has still not been spotted standing in line.

5/10/20

An anonymous source gave me a recording of a secret conclave with Governor Tom Wolf and his pack of advisors that was held at a hidden location in Intercourse, Pennsylvania.

Governor Wolf: Thank you all for coming today.

An Advisor: Marone! Couldja find a place more out in da boonies, boss?

Governor Wolf: Stop whining. We need to keep ultimate secrecy or the media might find out what we're doing.

An Advisor: And wad's wid da name of dis place? Do dey make porno here?

Governor Wolf: Fuggedaboutit!

An Advisor: Va bene.

Governor Wolf: Let's get down to business, starting with some old business. I'm still not happy with the colors we picked for our designated areas of the state. Red, yellow and green are so played. Everybody uses red, yellow and green, and they're too harsh. I think my original idea to go with mauve, salmon and chartreuse would have been much more effective at soothing the inmates … er, citizens. I think that would have made a better statement.

An Advisor: What? That we'se a bunch of pansies?

Governor Wolf: No, that we're sensitive and caring. My colors say empathy.

An Advisor: Your's colors say spank me.

Governor Wolf: Do you think it's too late to change them?

An Advisor: You's ain't gonna hold your's breath and stomp your's feet again, are you's?

Governor Wolf: Let's move on. I believe I did a pretty good job of quelling the disturbance at the Capitol by those gun-toting, Nazi, white supremacists.

An Advisor: Yeah, boss. Dat was great. Extendin' da stay-at-home order during da protest was beautiful.

Governor Wolf: That should keep them in line.

An Advisor: What'll happens if dey do it again?

Governor Wolf: I'll just keep extending the order ... like I did last week in the areas where those real estate thugs won't shut up.

A couple of advisors whisper to each other.

Advisor #1: What's wid da real estate guys?

Advisor #2: The boss don't like 'em.

Advisor #1: How come?

Advisor #2: Dey had an open house da boss wanted to see, but by da time he got dere, da cookies was all gone.

Governor Wolf: Any other business?

An Advisor: Da citizens are making lots a noise about da new statistics comin' out.

Governor Wolf: What statistics?

An Advisor: Da ones dat says almost 50 percent of all death in the country from da virus are from da New York an' Jersey metropolitan area. So's dey think we's safe here in P-A.

Governor Wolf: That's outrageous. I thought we were all on the same team here.

An Advisor: It gets worse, boss. Da stats say dat 70 percent of deaths here in P-A are in nursing homes.

Governor Wolf: Who the hell's putting out that crap? That's it! Get me a house painter ... or Hilary.

An Advisor: Dis stuff is dangerous, boss. Da natives is getting restless and threatenin' to open dere businesses in spite a you's orders. Wah we gonna do if dey do?

Governor Wolf: Arrest them! Throw them in jail!

The advisors look around the table at each other.

Governor Wolf: Why do you think I've been emptying the jails? Everybody laughs.

An Advisor: Yeah, boss. Li' Ant'ny, The Piano Wire and Sally the South Jersey Shovel are very grateful. Dey owes youse.

Governor Wolf: Someday — and that day may never come — I'll call upon them to do a service for me. But until that day, tell them to accept this justice as a gift. Capisce?

An Advisor: Will do, Capo dei capi.

Governor Wolf: In the meantime, let's keep the heat on. Now is no time to let up. A couple of more weeks with no toilet paper and we'll have them wearing tinfoil hats and sacrificing chickens.

Everybody laughs.

Governor Wolf: Next meeting is in two weeks in Blue Ball. Arrivederci.

5/11/20

I wanted to buy some Mother's Day flowers for my wife, but the florist shops are closed because it's too dangerous to be in a store with a few people, so I had to go to a grocery store with hundreds of people.

As a result of the closures, there are limited opportunities to conduct fundamental commerce in the enterprise of horticulture, so by the time I got to Wegmans, all the flowers were gone, not a posy posing anywhere.

Such is our strange new world.

Speaking of a strange new world, two of our sons moved out of the house in the last couple of weeks, defying the stay-at-home order. They had moved back in with us for a few months a couple of years ago, so their departure had been anticipated.

For a long, long time.

My wife had conversion plans for their bedrooms all ready, so as soon as the last box was moved out, she sent me to the hardware store to buy paint. It was on a weekend and I wanted to check the store's hours, so I went to its website and saw I had plenty of time to get there before it closed at 6 p.m. Alas, when I arrived at 5 p.m., they were locking up. Apparently they had changed their hours due to the coronavirus but hadn't updated the website. When I went back the next morning, I asked the owner why he changed the hours, and he said they were trying to reduce exposure to the virus.

"I guess business is off?" I asked.

"Oh, no," he replied. "We're busier than ever. Garden supplies are flying out the door, and I can't stock paint fast enough. Everybody's got time right now and they're fixing up their houses."

"So, business is up because of the lockdown?"

"Uh-huh," he said, and smiled.

"In other words, you're doing more business in fewer hours?"

"Right," he said, and leaned in and whispered, "and it's costing me less in wages and overhead." He straightened up and added, "To be honest with you, we were looking for a good time to reduce hours on the weekends, anyway."

"So, this has all worked out for you?" I asked.

"Yeah, I guess so."

"But you're putting more people in your store in a shorter time span, meaning there are now more people in the store all the time, increasing the risk of exposure," I reasoned.

"Oh, no," he said. "Everybody has to wear a face mask."

"Do you walk to work or carry your lunch?"

Nobody told me there'd be days like these. Strange days indeed — strange days indeed.

My bank changed its hours, too, and I found that out the hard way. I had to deposit a check into my business account to cover a check I'd written the day before. Yes, I know, it's called check kiting. I wrote about that subject in my book *Dancing in the Cave of the Dragon:*

"Banks make money by investing float. Float is the time span from when you make a deposit until the bank releases those funds into your account. It can take from one to five business days for those funds to be made available to you, and, in the meantime, the bank puts that money into short-term investments. That's called playing the float. (Sounds like a game at a casino, doesn't it? Now you're catching on.)

"When you play the float — writing a check you won't have to cover for a couple of days until it hits your bank — it's called check kiting, and banks don't like that. As a matter of fact, it's illegal and they can put you in jail for it. Woody Guthrie sang about Pretty Boy Floyd, the Robin Hood-like outlaw of the 1930s who had a penchant for robbing banks, 'Some will rob you with a six-gun and some with a fountain pen.' The difference being that they shoot you or put you in jail if you use a gun, but you a get a big house in the Hamptons if your weapon of choice is a pen."

Anyway, I got to the bank at 4:45 p.m. since it closes normally at 5 p.m. and since nobody told me of the change in hours. What a surprise. They charge $35 for overdrawn checks and that simple change of hours ended up costing me 70 smackeroos — I'm a slow learner. When I asked why they reduced their hours and are staffing the bank with only two people, the teller — through a window of thick, bulletproof acrylic and a cloth face mask with a cute kitten emblazoned across its width — just stared at me.

"I don't know," she finally said.

"But a reduction of hours makes no sense," I persisted. "The bank is still making money off its depositors and borrowers and they just got a bunch of money from the government to help them make even more money, and you have almost no contact with your customers, so how are any of these changes helping to protect anybody?"

"Well, we are wearing face masks," she offered.

"Do you live in a house or vacation in the mountains?"

Clowns to the left of me, jokers to the right; here I am, stuck in the middle with you.

5/12/20

We're living in in a paradox.

More people than ever are watching television, but the networks can't capitalize on the windfall by raising their advertising rates because people can't get out to buy and presently don't need their products or services. It's too bad for Tinseltown programmers because as we're working through this Gordian knot, people will watch almost any dreck they throw up there.

Like *Last Dance.* If you've missed the first eight episodes of this 10-episode boffo extravaganza (that's really all about we'll-watch-any-thing-related-to-sports-because-we're-jonesing-real-bad) piece of fluff, count yourself one of the lucky ones. Ostensibly, the show is about the career of basketball great Michael Jordan, but in reality it's about whitewashing Michael Jordon's dubious reputation. I wanted to wait until it was over to trash it, but it's gotten so bad I just couldn't resist. As a matter of fact, it's so bad I wasn't going to watch the last two episodes, but I'll watch anything related to sports because I'm jonesing real bad.

The show is on ESPN every Sunday night with two back-to-back episodes over five consecutive weeks. It ends next Sunday, and then we'll go back to watching reruns of the Eagles' Super Bowl beatdown of the Patriots in 2018 that never gets old and is infinitely more interesting, even after myriad viewings, than watching Jordan lace up his sneakers myriad times (apparently something the producers thought was of vital importance to the story line — or maybe just good filler in this moribund exercise of 21st century hyper-hype).

I was able to get ahold of next week's script where Jordan has to work through yet another traumatic experience that threatens to end his magnificent career. Before an important playoff game, Jordan discovers that he's out of deodorant, but all his lackeys and sycophants are out taking care of his myriad other needs, so Jordan has to actually go to the drugstore himself.

The horror!

If that wasn't bad enough, an old woman standing in line with Jordan at the cash register asks for an autograph.

One hardship after another!

Jordan has to draw on all his inner strength garnered from a lifetime of self-importance and recalcitrant narcissism to lead the Bulls to yet another phenomenal victory while breaking the record for sticking out your tongue while shooting.

Of course, as an alternative to network programming, you can watch the destruction, mayhem and total annihilation of all traditional family values on the streaming sites.

Good times.

Streaming is not something I've readily embraced. I come from a world where we didn't even have a TV until I was five, and then there were only three stations to choose from for many years, so I wasn't burdened with the Nonviable Vicarious Living Syndrome that plagues so much of society today. However, my monosyllabic son gave us an Amazon Fire TV Cube for Christmas, and I decided to hook it up this past Sunday in hopes of avoiding another episode of "Please, Please Love Me!"

Problem was, I couldn't open the damn remote control to insert the batteries, so I innocently called my son to ask if there was some secret, millennial trick to it. Unfortunately, he was with a horde of his monosyllabic, knuckle-dragging friends who were seriously libating. Instead of offering any help, they made fun of me, as if not being able to open the back of a remote control is some kind of early onset dementia. I reminded them that I had been putting batteries in remotes since before they were born, and, as a matter of fact, during my childhood I was the remote in our house. So I know remotes!

This is the same son who once compared me to Arthur Spooner from the TV show *The King of Queens*, but I'm going to fix his ass. Someday I'll move in with him and live in his basement.

Day 59 of Captivity

5/13/20

Things they do look awful c-c-cold — talkin' 'bout my generation. I hope I die before I get old — talkin' 'bout my generation.

Max Yasgur owned the farm in Bethel, New York, where the original Woodstock music festival was staged. I've had it in my head for some time now to write a book titled, *Max Yasgur's Dead*, about the difference between the Woodstock era and today's much more venomous climes. The social, economic, domestic and geopolitical issues that we faced during the Woodstock era, though serious and complex, seem like Civics 101 compared to where we are today with a cesspool of problems orchestrated to be so contentious that they defy resolution — the better to divide us and keep the oligarchy in power.

Certainly things weren't all groovy back in the 1960s and '70s, not with Vietnam, overt and systemic racial barriers, oppression of women and nontraditional lifestyles, assassinations, global unrest and really bad TV (unlike today when we have unbelievably bad TV), but we had something dearly missing in today's inclusive tapestry: hope. Oh, we have all manner of political hacks selling us hope, but I'm afraid old hope *caught the last train for the coast*, and in its place, left hate.

Hate — the hallmark of the beginning of the 21st century. And if you feel compelled to point a finger, first point it toward yourself. When it comes to hate, we truly are all in this together.

And along comes COVID-19 to bludgeon us with that edgy reality.

There's an article floating around on social media that claims Woodstock occurred during a pandemic, which, in accord with our current duality, is both true and untrue. It's true that between 1968 and 1969, the Hong Kong Flu (as we were allowed to call things what they were back in the day, before political correctness hampered our ability to effectively communicate) raged through the world, killing more than a million people, including over 100,000 right here in America.

Living in the U.S.A. ... Somebody give me a cheeseburger.

In this country, the average age of the dead was 65. Of course in those days, the average life span was only 70. At that time, the population was 200 million, which figures out to .05 percent of Americans died.

When all is said and done, our current pandemic will probably kill about 100,000 Americans, too. However, the average age of the dead this time around is over 80, and the average life span is up to 78. The population of the country today is about 330 million, which works out to .03 percent of the population succumbing to the virus.

A .02 percent aggregate gain, if all holds true.

Back then, many people who caught the flu died. Today, most people who catch the flu recover.

Back then, not a lot of people knew about the pandemic, and those who did paid almost no attention to it. Today, everybody knows about it and many people are cowering in the corner of their basements, shaking in fear.

Back then, nobody knew what narcissism meant and we pretty much took life as it came. Today, we are the embodiment of narcissism, and life better not mess with us or we'll sue its ass.

Back then, we weren't very aggressive in counting the dead. Today, don't lie down too long.

Back then, it was business as dysfunctionally usual. Today, what business? It left on that last train to the coast.

Back then, there was no social distancing. Today, don't you dare touch me with that thing … or anything else, either.

Back then, only criminals wore masks. Today, you can watch the criminals on the TV news shows and pontificating on C-SPAN, maskless.

Back then, you could go where you pleased. Today, the government tells you where to go (usually an anatomical impossibility).

What's not true about the Woodstock story is the implication that the pandemic was active during the summer of '69 — it wasn't — just like history suggests that our pandemic won't be this summer, even though the Weak-Kneed Willies of the world have taken over and are canceling most summer activities.

Back then, we liked having fun. Today, fun is the first syllable of fungus, and we are a fungus among us, living in the dark, decomposing our lives in fear of actually having to face the terror of living — not like it used to be when we robustly embraced life, trepidations and all. We were mellower then, and I'll bet if that Hong Kong Flu had shown up at Woodstock, it would've smoked a doob, got naked and kicked back.

I'm going on down to Yasgur's farm,
I'm going to join in a rock 'n' roll band.
I'm going to camp out on the land,
I'm going to try an' get my soul free.

5/14/20

Welcome to Friday morning, which used to be a big deal.

Fridays don't have the same cachet they once held when we were all part of the fabric of American commerce, but that fabric has badly frayed, and weekends are now just another couple of days. That said, I still like weekends. I write these provocative essays Monday through Friday to give myself some semblance of normalcy, to reestablish borders and help create a bit of that old excitement for the end of the week (as if writing my little slices of life for you isn't exciting as all get out).

So, go ahead, get out!

But before you do, here are a few tidbits from the news you may have missed this past week, as prologued by Billy Joel. *Say goodbye to Hollywood. Say goodbye my baby.* Nestled in the opulence and glamor of Hollywood lurks danger.

Remember Stanley Roper? How about Adam Cartwright? Spearchucker Jones?

The list goes on and on, all characters on television sitcoms that disappeared without a trace — one day part of a beloved cast of characters, the next, gone with the wind, never to be heard from again. Stanley Roper was the lecherous landlord on *Three's Company* who had no interest in his wife's incessant sexual advances. After a few seasons, they both disappeared into the ether, forever frozen in a conundrum of unrequited/unwelcomed love.

Adam Cartwright was the oldest son of Ben Cartwright in the original cast of *Bonanza*, the first TV show I saw in color, although color in this context is a gross exaggeration — it was more like eerily vague tinting. One day, Adam rode off the Ponderosa for parts unknown and happy trails to you.

Spearchucker Jones was a black surgeon on *M*A*S*H*, whose name was intended to be funny but was beyond a macro-transgression even in 1972. The first time I heard it, I did a double take. Fortunately for America's fragile racial sensibilities, Jones vanished into thin air, never again to chuck the spear of bigotry.

Probably the most famous Hollywood Houdini was Chuck Cunningham, Richie Cunningham's older brother on *Happy Days*. Not only did Chuck go gently into that good night, so did a second Chuck. Two Chucks, both evaporated like the last vestige of yesterday's coffee at the bottom of your cup.

As astonishing as it is to believe, this week Governor Gavin Newsom of California announced that the bodies of all those missing characters had been located in a shack at the back of an old studio lot. Remarkably, they had all died from COVID-19.

We all have a face that we hide away forever.

Well, hide your face no more! Dr. Fauci, the esteemed expert on contradiction, told the country that we should not wear masks.

I kid you not. The guy actually said that. In this dramatic week of unmasking, we may now unmask.

What can I add? I'm just breathing into this bag trying to stop hyperventilating.

Mama, if that's movin' up then I'm movin' out.

Pennsylvania's Health Secretary, Dr. Rachel Levine, moved her mother out of a nursing home while instructing nursing homes to accept patients suffering from COVID-19. As a result of that order, 70 percent of deaths from the virus in Pennsylvania have been in nursing homes.

If I made this stuff up, you wouldn't believe me.

Many well-educated and well-respected medical experts are telling us that a lot of the measures we've adopted to fight the coronavirus have been useless window dressing, but you'll have a difficult time hearing them because they've been silenced by the new normal. Dr. Levine, on the other hand, whom you get to hear all the time, wants to keep us locked down and away from each other and our livelihoods until such a time when her mother is completely safe.

I don't know, in a time of crisis when you need information and advice from folks who have spent their lives studying infectious diseases,

I'm not sure I want a pediatrician calling the shots.

Maybe it's just me.

And maybe it won't be long until come on, babe, and take me away. We got some money to spend tonight.

5/17/20

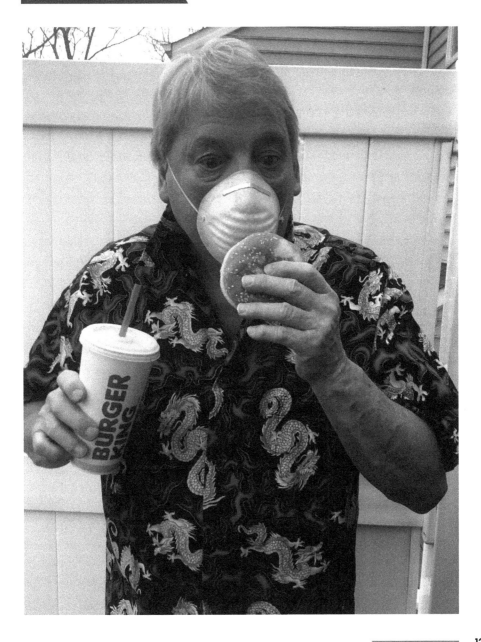

I hear we're getting another stimulus check from Uncle Sam, and I didn't even drink televangelist Peter Popoff's miracle spring water. During this time of national emergency, I wouldn't bother drinking miracle spring water anyway because it contains none of the miracle stuff I'm looking for: calories! As everybody knows, the best way to fight COVID-19 is to consume as much foodstuff as possible, the higher in sugar and fat content, the better. Accordingly, here at Calories R Us we have a saying: If it ain't inflatin', we ain't relatin'. You know, if things keep going like this, I'll soon be consulting Mama June for some weight-loss tips.

I never eat fast food, not only because it is so fattening and unhealthy, but mostly because it upsets my tummy (as I'm a sensitive and delicate person, and before you say anything, tequila's different — it's made from the agave plant, so it's a vegetable). But this new and opportunistic coronavirus has changed all that.

Like today when I visited my son at his new apartment in New Jersey. He wanted me to help him put up curtain rods in the living room and bedrooms, so I drove the hour to his place in what northern Jerseyans call Central Jersey, but those of us from South Jersey, who know what's what, call North Jersey with a heavy inflection on New York City. We worked for a couple of hours on the installations without much difficulty, and then I headed back to my home of choice, Pennsylvania, which isn't North, Central or South Jersey, although we do have diners and, believe it or not, we're putting in traffic circles.

Talk about retrograde!

I was starving, and since there were almost no other places in the Garden State to stop and grab a quick in-between-meal snack (that happened to be between breakfast and brunch), I decided to stop at Micky D's. Because of said lack of alternatives, I've been eating the occasional fast food in-between-meal snack a few times a day, and I'm afraid I've not only built up a tolerance to synthetic unnourishment, I also believe my taste buds have died.

Remember when fast food was fast? Not anymore, Jack and Jackettes.

Everybody must have had the same idea I did since every McDonald's I passed had a long line of cars snaking through its parking lots. I didn't feel like spending the rest of my morning in one of those insufferable lines, so I kept moving along, hoping to find a more accessible grease emporium. I was having no luck until I finally found a Burger King with only five cars in line. After a short wait, I drove up to a monolith with a speaker in the middle.

"What can we get for you?" the monolith asked.

I ordered a spicy chicken sandwich in hopes of finding my lost palate.

"Will that be a meal?"

I replied yes, and the monolith asked what I'd like to drink.

"I'll have a bottle of water, please."

"I'm sorry, we're out of water. How about a diet drink instead?"

"So, what? You don't think the food's going to do a good enough job poisoning me?"

"How about a Coke, then?" the monolith suggested.

"No Coke, Pepsi?" I said in my finest John Belushi Billy Goat Tavern accent.

Silence from the monolith.

"I'll have a Coke, please," I said.

The monolith told me what I owed and asked me to pull up to the first window, and then added, "Please wear a mask while at the window."

"Pardon me?"

"You need to cover your mouth and nose while at the windows," it instructed. "We're trying to protect our employees."

"Is it okay if I take the mask off while I eat?" I asked.

"Of course," the monolith responded.

"Did Governor Murphy say that's okay?"

"Why would Governor Murphy expect you to eat while wearing a mask?"

"Well, I heard he agreed with Governor Newsom from California who said it's okay to walk on the beach as long as you stay on the wet sand, but stay off the dry sand. Now, I'm no physicist, but for the life of me, I can't figure out how you can get to the wet sand without walking on the dry sand, so telling us to eat while wearing masks doesn't seem like too much of a stretch, does it?"

"Please move along," the monolith said.

5/18/20

"Caution: If a piano falls on your head, you may be in danger of dying from COVID-19."

Cute, eh? I saw that on Facebook this morning and it made me laugh. It's funny because we are being bombarded with so much information — most of it contradictory — that we've reached a point where we believe almost anything's possible.

Or nothing is, and we're starting to question everything we're being told.

That's probably where I'm at right about now. Whatever the nattering nabobs of negativism or ponderous purveyors of pomposity tell me, my first reaction is to become a Missourian: Show me!

Like with the coronavirus death count. While some say it's being inflated for the political gain of influence and control, others counter that it's being underreported and we all should be hiding under our beds. I say we have no idea what the real number is and never will because speaking with forked tongue, or at least with a serious emphasis on hyperbole, is standard procedure for advancement in the world of "Now you see it, now you don't."

So, as a public service, here are some facts.

Fact No. 1: Lots of people die

Fact No. 2: from lots of things

Fact No.3: and you can't do anything about it.

You may be able to change the trajectory, but you can't change the hard landing. It's always tragic to someone, and it's always a pain you're powerless to mitigate, so do the best you can and move on.

All this whinin' and cryin' and pitchin' a fit — get over it, get over it.

Hope that helps.

And while you're moving on, try to be nice about it.

Remember when this whole mess started, back when it was a medical emergency, before it became a societal issue and politically expedient, when people were frightened and compliant and amazingly cooperative?

Well, that train's left the station and ain't comin' back soon!

Trouble ahead, trouble behind. And you know that notion just crossed my mind.

And in its place, left behind plenty of anger and defiance.

I learned that the other day on my foray into the wilderness of New Jersey. Not that New Jersey is any different from anyplace else these days, but for me, going outside of my it's-a-small-world-after-all felt like going where no man has gone before. You see, folks, it had been almost 10 weeks since I had traveled any farther than the hardware store — about five miles away — so my trepidatious excursion was a real adventure into the unknown.

And it wasn't all that pleasant being back out on the road.

I wish that I knew what I know now.

The first thing I noticed was that almost everybody was on their cellphone, and they were shouting into them. They looked mad, and nasty, and they kept shooting me dirty looks.

Was it something I said?

Driving on Interstate 78 felt like Saturday afternoon at Dorney Park's bumper cars. People were swerving in and out of traffic lanes without any indication of their intentions (that were pure evil, I was sure) because, apparently, everybody's turn signals were broken. And if I didn't get out of the way fast enough, I got flipped off.

It was such a lovely spring day and I couldn't count all the birds.

Aggressions were in the red phase with less chance of going yellow than Governor Tom Wolf answering a question. Road rage gone wild was the theme of the day.

And speaking of Tom Wolf and his brethren, that unbridled hostility reminded me of the old definition of stress: "The confusion created when one's mind overrides the body's basic desire to choke the living shit out of some asshole who desperately deserves it."

Up ahead in the distance, I saw a shimmering light.

And speaking of Tom Wolf, I spotted an open liquor store in

Phillipsburg, New Jersey — the last stop before returning to Wolf's Lair. I went in and bought some gin and rum that are nearly impossible to get in Pennsylvania and was amazed at how crowded the place was for a Sunday morning. And guess what? Almost all the cars in the parking lot had PA tags. I wonder how much that's costing the commonwealth in lost revenue and taxes.

You put your head in
You put your head out
You put your head in
And you bang it all about
You do the hokey pokey
And you turn yourself around
That's what it's all about

5/19/20

In a world where "fat chance" and "slim chance" mean the same thing, is it any wonder we're having so much trouble communicating, especially now with the added pressure of this invasively influential influenza? So to help out, here's a glossary of terms being used during this break between investigations and impeachments.

•**Coronavirus:** A virus named after a Mexican beer because it makes you feel the same way you do after a night of Mexican beer and tequila. (Apparently, coronatequilavirus was too long.)

•**COVID-19:** The disease you get from the coronavirus. Soon it will be a streamed show titled "Unsolved Mysteries of the 21st Century: Hoax or End of the World as We Know It?"

•**Epidemic:** Lots of people getting sick from the same thing, usually the result of watching too many streamed shows.

•**Pandemic:** A disease that everybody in the world is vulnerable to except Keith Richards.

•**Draconian:** A verbal space-filler overused by cognitively impaired, linguistics-challenged newscasters.

•**Unprecedented Times:** Dramatic effect to camouflage vapid stupidity.

•**New Normal:** A term that has absolutely no meaning at all. Ignore it while giving the person using it a look of incredulous disbelief (although they won't be able to see it through your face mask, so you might want to add a disgruntled grunt).

•**Medical Experts:** No such thing. Pasteboard props used by cable news programs.

•**Underlying Condition:** Stuff people worked hard their entire lives to get.

•**Hypertension:** High blood pressure, but hypertension sounds so much cooler. Comes from watching too many cable news programs.

•**Epidemiologists:** Doctors who appear on cable news shows to give you hypertension.

•**Obesity:** Look in the mirror.

•**Stay-at-Home Orders:** How I spent my teenage years.

•**Social Distancing:** A practice of standing six feet apart so you don't spit on other people.

•**Face Masks:** Masks covering people's mouths and noses, made of different materials and constructed in various configurations, some extremely creative, but all full of disgusting crud and nasty germs from being worn for two months. Maintain social distancing anytime you see one. Actually, you're better off running away.

•**Washing Hands:** Something we learned when we were two years old, but apparently not well enough for the overlords. The modern method of hand washing is to vigorously wash for "long time, Joe," until you've killed any chance of building up immunity to anything.

•**Hand Sanitizer:** Greatly improves your chance of getting sick because it destroys your immune system. Cleanliness truly is next to godliness because if you keep using that life-inhibiting potion, you're going to meet God real soon.

•**Shaking Hands:** Fuhgeddaboudit.

•**Human Touch:** A Bruce Springsteen song.

•**Dancing:** We got lucky on this one, guys. Next time she tries to drag you onto the dance floor, just say, "Social distancing, Babe."

•**Sex:** No need. Our politicians are taking care of that for us.

Day 66 of Captivity

5/20/20

Dr. Rachel Levine, Secretary of Health for the Commonwealth of Pennsylvania, has not only been guiding Governor Tom Wolf and his administration through the whitewater of the coronavirus crisis, but has also been counseling the governor on a more personal level. After having spent years working in the field of adolescent psychiatry, she certainly has the credentials. Let's listen in to yesterday's session.

Dr. Levine: You must be feeling better now that you have those real estate people off your back.

Governor Wolf: Those bastards! They ate my cookies!

Dr. Levine: Now, Tommy, we've talked all through that. Yes, your mommy made those cookies for you. And yes, she set them out to cool while you had to leave the house so that the real estate agent could show your home to prospective buyers. And yes, the real estate agent let those prospective buyers eat all your cookies. It was a tragic situation, no doubt, but you've worked so hard to overcome it, and setting the real estate people free so they can make a living is a tremendous step in the right direction.

Governor Wolf: I want my cookies!

Dr. Levine: You had to do it, Tommy. It was the right thing to do.

Governor Wolf: Big deal. I was giving them plenty of free money in unemployment benefits to stay home. I don't get this need to work and make money. Why couldn't they go to their mumsy and daddy for more money?

Dr. Levine: Not everybody has that advantage.

Governor Wolf: I know, I know. That's why I'm sneaking a $15 minimum wage into Phase Three. For six years I've been trying to get that passed, but like they say, you never want a serious crisis to go to waste. Those greedy business owners can afford it, just like I could've when I was running my old and extremely successful family business, only the time wasn't quite right then. Why don't people love me?

Dr. Levine: Those polls you prefer say most Pennsylvanians are happy with you.

Governor Wolf: They ought to be happy with me. It's costing a lot of money for them to be happy with me. I'm even letting them commit fraud by refusing to go back to work and keep collecting. Everybody's talking about how hard they have it. We know all about how hard it is, don't we? I mean, the two of us are barely scraping by on $350,000 a year. And that's between us, for goodness sake.

Dr. Levine: What's bothering you today, Tommy? You look troubled.

Governor Wolf: I'm worried about my legacy. I've worked so hard to gain complete control over the state — I can do whatever I want and make people do whatever I want them to do. There's nothing quite as pleasing as seeing signs that read, "Closed by order of Gov. Tom Wolf." It's fun, but I only have two years left to enjoy it. Somebody else is going to walk in here, distort and manipulate an emergency and get to use all my powers. It's not fair!

Dr. Levine: Life's not always fair, Tommy. Didn't you learn that when you got all those degrees from fancy schools and ended up a cabinet maker?

Governor Wolf: I have an idea for how to seal my reputation as a great leader.

Dr. Levine: What's that?

Governor Wolf: This woman on Long Island, Nassau County Executive Laura Curran, has banned playing doubles tennis. You can play singles, but you can't touch other people's balls. Got that? She said, "You can kick their balls, but you can't touch them." She also said, "To avoid confusion between whose balls are whose, you can use a marker like a Sharpie to mark out with an X and put someone's initials on them."

What a great idea; marking your balls so that no one else can touch them. Well, I have a better idea. How about if I banned playing tennis with any balls at all? You'd have to use your imagination to see the ball and react to the other player's swing. It would be great for developing virtual recreation, and eventually, virtual living. I can see it growing and becoming a movement, and I would have started it all.

I would forever be known as the no-balls governor.

Day 67 of Captivity

5/21/20

If you watch much TV, you're being inundated with commercials thanking first responders, police and medical workers for their sacrifices during the pandemic.

Not that those folks don't deserve our gratitude and support, but I find all the displays of appreciation somewhat self-serving. It's like the advertisers are trying to glom onto the altruism, subliminally telling us what great people they are because they recognize the work of great people. Look, we all know how valuable these front-liners are and how much we depend on their courage and skills, but please hold the covert messages for tooth whiteners, adult diapers and ultrasoft toilet paper that we so long for. It's a wee bit opportunistic and disingenuous, don't you think?

And I want my fair share.

So, here are a few people I'd like to thank for their contributions to the joys of hermitude, starting with the United States Postal Service. Neither snow nor rain nor heat nor gloom of night nor germs of a nefarious nature stay these couriers from the swift completion of stuffing crap into your regulation, undersized mailbox.

It all started when I leased a new Ford Escape about a year ago. I was set to sign the papers for a white, Titanium model with all the bells and whistles when another salesman from the dealership parked a sleek, midnight gray Escape with bitchin' black rims in front of the showroom window where I was sitting.

Stop the presses!

I really didn't care about a lot of bells and whistles as much as I cared about looking cool, and I would look prettttttty, prettttttty cool in that baby (but you be the judge of that). The reason I was getting the Escape in the first place was because it had a keypad on the door so I wouldn't have to carry my keys with me when I went hiking or biking or skiing or bebopping around town looking prettttttty, prettttttty cool. My only regret in taking the youthful, swinging sports model instead of the practical, old man Titanium was that I didn't get a built-in GPS, but I figured I could use my iPad. Problem was, the iPad wouldn't sit still anywhere in the car, so, with too much time on my hands, I finally ordered a nifty iPad bracket from Walmart that allegedly fits into a cup holder.

Unfortunately, the box it came in was a hair bigger than my mailbox, so the dedicated postal worker made it fit.

Want to guess how he did that?

When I opened my mailbox, it was jammed in so tight I couldn't get the damn thing out without tearing apart the box. And it's a good thing the mailman destroyed the box because the damn thing didn't fit into the cup holder as advertised, and I had to take the damn thing back to Walmart together with the torn box and get a refund for the damn thing delivered in a damaged box.

Thank you, Mr. Neither Snow nor Rain nor yadda yadda yadda.

I'd also like to thank my garbage men. They have been taking such care during the quarantine that I haven't had to sweep up any broken bottles for almost two months.

How nice.

Now, if they would actually empty the trash cans instead of leaving them half full, I'd be delighted. Oh well, I guess the new normal has retained some of the values of the old normal.

And how about a big shout out to the security guard at my home away from home, Wegmans? His job is to stand in the entrance like a doorman at a hip, New York discothèque and decide who gets in and who doesn't. He also makes sure you're wearing a mask, and one day I forgot to put on mine. He reminded me as I entered the store and seemed so happy to have had to reprimand me because, apparently, everybody else is better at following the rules and he never gets the opportunity to reprimand anybody. So now I make him reprimand me every time I visit the place just to keep him happy. It's my small contribution of support for our valuable support personnel.

And while I'm at it, thank you very much LightInTheBox for holding my $80.22 for seven weeks before informing me that the fancy, digital thermometer I ordered was out of stock. Hope you made some nice change off the float.

Same to you, officefurniture.com. Thank you, thank you, thank you for hanging onto my $202.26 for safekeeping while I've patiently awaited the desk I ordered three weeks ago but won't get until July. And a special thank you for condescendingly insisting that you had informed me of the delay in an email, but when you resent the email, there was no mention of the delay.

Surprise, surprise, surprise!

On a more serious note, please allow me to step out of character for a moment to thank my youngest son's girlfriend, Andi Wilkinson. She's a nurse who works on the COVID-19 ward at Overlook Medical

Center in Summit, New Jersey, where she's had to deal with the virus every day. To most of us, COVID-19 is a concept, or maybe a small threat, but to Andi and her co-workers, and to the countless other medical staffs around the country and the world, it's very real and immediate. It may only affect a small percentage of the population, but watching that small percentage of infected people in excruciating pain and dying alone is an experience most of us couldn't handle.

I stand in awe of you, Andi.

5/25/20

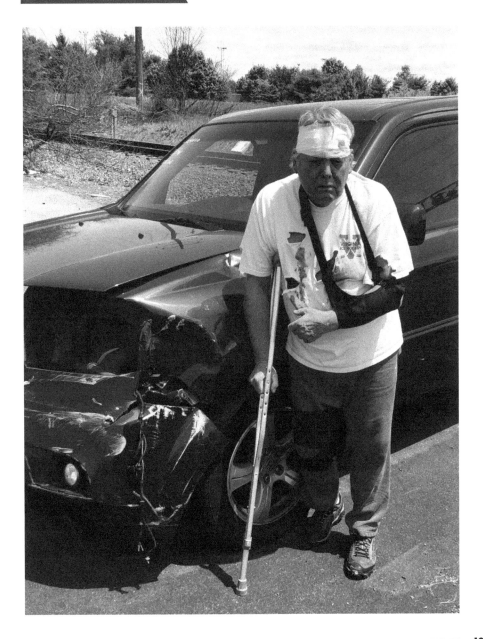

Will Rogers said, "When I die, I want to die like my grandfather, who died peacefully in his sleep. Not screaming like all the passengers in his car."

You've probably heard that one before, but it's still kind of funny, right? Funny in an interesting, macabre sort of way because your chances of dying in a car crash are only 0.94 percent.

Here's a list of chances of dying from some other humorous causes.

- **Heart disease:** 16.7 percent.

- **Cancer:** 14.3 percent.

- **Suicide:** 1.7 percent.

- **Opiate overdose:** 1 percent.

- **Falls:** 0.9 percent.

- **COVID-19:** 0.03 percent (although some will argue 0.04 percent, or the really hopeful might go as high as 0.05 percent). What that means, folks, is that you are twice as likely to die in your shower than you are of COVID-19.

And it's time to do something about that threat to mankind. From now on, there will be no showering by anyone at any time. The police may come into your home and forcibly remove your shower cap, loofah and rubber ducky, by order of whoever is trying to get their party elected in November. And no more motor vehicles, either — from henceforth, there will be no driving. We're done with all you selfish, insensitive people getting into your cars every day and KILLING PEOPLE!!!

Look, nobody with any brains thinks the coronavirus is a hoax, and they know it's very real and very deadly, just like a lot of other stuff, only much more aggressively at this time. On the other hand, anybody with a brain knows we're being misled and misinformed, sometimes out of ignorance and inexperience with the virus, and sometimes on purpose in order to continue to manipulate and abuse us — you know, how we like it: "Thank you, sir, may I have another."

Don't believe me? Try these facts on for size, buster: The United States makes up four percent of the world's population, but we are being told that we have 32 percent of the world's cases of COVID-19 within our borders, and that a whopping 28 percent of deaths resulting from the disease is ours, too. That means, hands down, we lead the world in lying about the coronavirus.

We're number one! We're number one!

What? You believe those statistics?

In that case: Boy, do I have a deal for you.

I happen to have in my possession a limited number of three-ounce bottles of the actual mud that was once under the feet of someone who was at Woodstock. Only $19.95 for this one-of-a-kind keepsake, along with a certificate of authenticity guaranteeing that the bottles contain real mud. Act now and receive a genuine, extinguished roach from a member of the Woodstock Nation, collected at his retirement home by a certified exterminator.

Seriously, do you ever feel like a rat in a maze looking for the cheese?

Well here's another clue for you all. The walrus was Paul.

Which of course was a lie; the walrus was John, as they keep moving the cheese and telling us the walrus was Paul.

Steve Thode, a professor emeritus of finance at Lehigh University, knows his walruses. In a piece printed in my local newspaper, The Morning Call, he takes Pennsylvania to task for moving the cheese. The following are a few excerpts from his article:

"I have been tracking the daily reports on COVID-19 cases and deaths from the Pennsylvania Department of Health [since] March ...

"I soon began to realize that the data the Department of Health was providing was terribly flawed. For example, on numerous occasions, the DoH would report counties that had a negative number of new cases. Impossible!

"And then the DoH began to list not only confirmed new COVID-19 cases and new deaths, but also 'probable' new COVID-19 cases and deaths. The DoH provided no guidance on exactly what a 'probable' case or 'probable' death is.

"What is a 'probable' case? I thought COVID-19 tests came back either 'positive' or 'negative.' Apparently, the DoH has created a third result called, 'Um, we're not sure...'

"Remarkably, the Pennsylvania media have widely ignored these data problems and simply report the DoH data without question often inaccurately. Perhaps they would be a little more curious if they were shut down, like thousands of small business owners who, day-by-day, are losing hope of ever recovering."

It's a well-reasoned and effectively articulated perspective that I recommend you Google and read. In the meantime, never forget for a moment that the good people telling you to stay home and not to worry about losing everything have not lost one single paycheck or forfeited any of their lavish benefits. I'm sure they get a good laugh about it over gin and tonics at their manors in the Hamptons.

> *Expert, texpert choking smokers,*
> *Don't you think the joker laughs at you*
> *(ho ho ho, hee hee hee, hah hah hah).*
> *See how they smile like pigs in a sty,*
> *see how they snide.*

5/26/20

This is outrageous!
This is heresy!
This is the last straw!

They've canceled the Riverton, New Jersey, Fourth of July Parade!

I grew up in a little town across the Delaware River from North Philadelphia. The town had no agricultural industry, no manufacturing to speak of, no large retail base (except the small shops along and near Main Street), no nothing except the Norman Rockwell–like houses peacefully squatting beneath its bountiful and prodigious trees, lining the peaceful streets in their correct orderliness. Riverton, New Jersey, had almost no identity at all … except the Fourth of July Parade.

And now they've canceled that identity, erased the ageless spectacle of affirmation that life can stand still, crushed one of the last vestiges of my bilateral childhood under the hobnailed boots of manic oppression.

The bastards!

What's next? Thanksgiving? Christmas? Boxing Day?

The bastards!

And so, here we find ourselves again, still in the midst of this draconian and unprecedented house arrest, relegated to watching the most inane and artless shows on my newfangled Amazon Fire TV Cube, eating and eating and then some more eating … and bitching.

Don't forget bitching.

Pet Peeve No.13

Please explain to me Home Depot on Saturday mornings. The line to get in runs around the building to the loading docks at the back of the store. I'm confused — isn't every day Saturday in the new normal? So, wassup? *'Cause if my eyes don't deceive me, there's something going wrong around here.* Maybe more people are working than they're letting on. Or, maybe people are victims of habit. And what the hell is wrong with me? Why am I going to Home Depot on Saturday mornings? Oh, that's right. I'm busy during the week writing these provocative essays.

Pet Peeve No.14

I hear Elon Musk wants to live on Mars. I thought he already did.

When you go, Elon, please take along Mark Zuckerberg, Bill Gates, Jeff Bezos … and let's throw in Mark Cuban, too. All you tech billionaires who got filthy rich turning folks into barely functioning zombies, maybe Mars is the perfect place for you. There, in a vacuum of lifeless aloneism (remember high school?), you guys can set the stratum, become the men you never could be here on Earth where you've proven the Beatles wrong. It's not love you can't buy, is it, boys?

I don't care too much for money. Money can't buy me COOL!

But on Mars, maybe each of you can reach your wildest dreams and be *the heaviest cat, the heaviest cat you ever did see.*

Cool jerks, indeed!

Pet Peeve No.15

And what's with the people in parking lots walking behind my car as I'm backing out. Don't they see my backup lights? Don't they see my car moving backwards, toward them in a menacing manner? Is the new normal that people are as stupid as they were in the old normal? Of course, it's hard to see anything when your head's buried up your ass in electronic pretend-life. Yo, Elon and the Synapses Abductors! I hear Mars calling.

Pet Peeve No.16

This is interesting: The grocery stores don't want you using your reusable bags. They say the bags are full of germs.

Ooooooo, germs!

Instead, they want you to use their plastic throwaways. You know, the ones that were persona non grata yesterday?

> *Don't throw the past away*
> *You might need it some rainy day*
> *Dreams can come true again*
> *When everything old is new again*

It used to be that you could take back your collected plastic bags, but the grocery stores have removed the plastic-bag recycling bins. They say the bags carry germs.

Ooooooo, germs!

Wow, all those bags blowing in the wind and going out to sea. I fear bad days ahead for Flipper and SpongeBob SquarePants.

Pet Peeve No.17

Speaking of "they say," they say that muscle weighs more than fat.

Really?

Well, I say they're wrong because I've been diligently replacing muscle with fat for the past 10 weeks and my weight hasn't gone down a gram. Apparently, the new normal is that fat most definitely outweighs muscle.

Either that or my scale's broken. Yeah, let's go with that.

Pet Peeve No.18

The blood banks are screaming for blood, especially mine because I'm a universal donor. I called on April 6 and was given an appointment for June 25. Desperate, eh?

That new normal — I just can't keep up with it.

5/27/20

Becky's Drive-In movie theater is a landmark in Northampton County, Pennsylvania, and was cited in 2016 in USA Today's 10 Best Drive-In Theaters. Becky's also was recognized for "The Best of the Best" in Showmanship by the Drive-In Theater Fan Club in 1996 and was included in the *New York Times'* "*10 Drive-Ins Worth a Detour.*" The place is a treasure here in the Lehigh Valley, as is Shankweiler's Drive-In Theatre, not too far down the road, the oldest operational drive-in theater in the United States.

While our kids were growing up, we spent many pleasant summer evenings at those drive-ins, sleeping peacefully during the second feature, which was a lot different from my teenage years, visiting the local "passion pits" definitely not to sleep … or to watch the movie, for that matter. Autos must have had really bad ventilation systems back then because those car windows were always steamed up.

So, I was pleased to hear that Becky's was reopening last weekend, in spite of Herr Wolf's unilateral and illegal order to stay closed. They had retrofitted the old place in accordance with accepted safety measures for protection against the coronavirus, such as cars parking nine feet apart and cleaning the restrooms after each use. In other words, they were acting like responsible and thoughtful adults who didn't need to be told where to sit and when to speak, like a bunch of callow kindergarteners. Unfortunately, the Gestapo showed up and closed them down with the threat of der Führer pulling their license to operate.

It's too bad Becky's doesn't make kitchen cabinets.

In perhaps the best example ever of the pot calling the kettle black, Governor Tom Wolf called people cowards who opened their businesses against his demands. This is the same guy who hides behind his usurped power and won't tell anybody what he's doing, why he's doing it and to whom he is doing it. This is the same guy who abetted the deaths of countless nursing home residents by ordering homes to accept people diagnosed with the coronavirus, while telling business owners trying to preserve their livelihoods that their irresponsible actions would cost lives.

Thank God we have the watchdog media … oh, that's right, they were busy cashing their paychecks.

Casey would waltz with the strawberry blonde, and the band played on.

If you enjoyed Gabe Kapler destroying the Philadelphia Phillies baseball team by using analytics, then you're going to love Tom Wolf destroying the lives of millions of Pennsylvanians using the same weapon. This guy Wolf probably goes to the bathroom on a system of metrics and probabilities. Like Kapler, Wolf doesn't seem capable of making common-sense decisions. Truly, he doesn't seem to have any common sense or the cognitive ability to reason.

In other words, he's a dope who has spent his entire life trying to cover it up.

Well, Mr. Governor, here's some reasoning you will probably find difficult, if not impossible, to understand:

According to The Hill, "Health experts say people are significantly less likely to get the coronavirus while outside … experts are increasingly confident in evidence showing that the coronavirus spreads much more readily indoors than outdoors."

Hear that, gub'na? "EVIDENCE SHOWING!" Isn't evidence an analytic without a fancy degree?

Maybe you'll listen to a guy with a title, if that helps. Scott Gottlieb, M.D., the former federal Food and Drug Administration commissioner, wrote, "Studies suggest activities held outdoors as temperatures warm pose lower COVID risk than those done in confined indoor spaces,"

Still don't believe it? Okay, then take it from a fellow demigod (and this is from CNBC, one of your faves): "Most new COVID-19 hospitalizations in New York state are from people who were staying home and not venturing much outside, a 'shocking' finding, Gov. Andrew Cuomo said."

How's that for shooting the hell out of your stay-in-power-enabling analytics?

Here's a little news for you, Tommy Baby: BECKY'S DRIVE-IN IS

OUTSIDE!

Of course, analytics dictate that keeping folks locked up and more vulnerable to the virus would greatly help facilitate a coup d'état.

Got to give us what we want
Gotta give us what we need
Our freedom of speech is freedom or death
We got to fight the powers that be

5/28/20

Governor Tom Wolf of Pennsylvania began his press conference on Friday, May 22, by removing his facemask, washing his hands with sanitizer, adjusting his glasses with both hands while being careful not to touch his face, and then destroyed the whole illusion by opening his mouth.

What a show. All that was missing was a big red ball on his nose and an oversized lapel flower spurting water.

Send in the clowns. Don't bother, they're here.

One of the first things he said was, "… we succeeded in slowing the growth [of the coronavirus] by our actions, our collective decisions to stay at home and avoid social contact; we know that all that saved lives."

Does this man have no shame?

Didn't he arbitrarily and unilaterally send numerous seniors into harm's way? Setting aside that bit of fatal judgment for the moment, how does he know that we saved lives?

He quoted a Drexel University study that employed the age-old scientific investigative method of eye of newt and toe of frog to determine that staying at home has saved a gazillion lives. Problem is, there is not a scintilla of empirical evidence to support such a claim, only propositions supported by suppositions based on flawed models that have been discredited by everybody but the media. And there's not a scintilla of proof to support the stuff Wolf lays out as sacrosanct. His entire plan has been constructed out of chewing gum, chicken wire and "Gosh, I hope this works."

We don't know if any of the myriad and painful sacrifices we've made have had any effect on the spread of the virus because there is no way of determining what could have happened with any kind of certainty. Anybody with half a brain knows that you can't measure what didn't happen. Unfortunately, I think we're going to come up half a brain short on this one.

What we do know, though — what empirical evidence we do have — comes from a comparison with Sweden, which employed practically none of Wolf's draconian measures during these unprecedented times, yet didn't lose a gazillion people as predicted by said disclaimed models and Tom Terrific. Here in the United States, we have 514 cases of COVID-19 to every 100,000 people, while Sweden only has 345 cases to a 100,000. Sweden's death rate per thousand is slightly higher than ours, but keep in mind the median age in the U.S. is 38.1, and in Sweden it's 41.2. In other words, Sweden has an older population than we do, and as we've learned (because people under 65 have a 99.infinity chance of surviving the disease), the coronavirus almost exclusively attacks the elderly.

A fact that renders the comparison to the 1918 Spanish flu somewhat unsuitable. That virus was less discriminating and attacked people of all ages, including children, which our virus, for the most part, doesn't. Record keeping in those days wasn't as sophisticated as it is today (where we've refined the system to maybes, could-bes and I sure want it-to-bes), so most of the numbers from the 1918 pandemic are speculative, at best.

The general use of the Spanish flu relative to the coronavirus is the comparison between how Philadelphia reacted compared to St. Louis's response. It is believed that the Spanish flu entered the United States through the Philadelphia Naval Yard where thousands of sailors and soldiers were returning home from Europe and World War I, bringing with them the deadly virus. Once the virus was discovered, Philadelphia didn't shut down for two weeks. The virus is believed to have reached St. Louis through an army base just outside the city, and St. Louis shut down almost immediately. A lot of people died in both places, but considerably more in Philadelphia.

At first blush (and does anybody ever go past first blush any longer, or even know what "at first blush" means?), that's pretty damning evidence that stay-at-home orders work, but a closer examination of the facts (something we're loath to do in modern times) paints a different picture. To begin, Philadelphia's population, including transient labor in town for the war effort, was more than two million, while St. Louis was less than half the size with a population of 750,000. The flu came to Philadelphia unexpectedly and spread rapidly before anybody knew what was going on, but by the time it reached St. Louis, everybody pretty much knew what was happening and, accordingly, had time to react and prepare. In Philadelphia, many people, especially workers, lived in overcrowded, squalid conditions, whereas St. Louis had better natural spacing between people. Because of those conditions, and regardless of almost any precautions (and just like New York City in our version of death by foreign invasion), Philadelphia was going to lose a lot more people than St. Louis simply because it was Philadelphia, so to extrapolate certain elements of the story to fit a narrative is sophistry.

But I know the neighborhood and talk is cheap when the story is good, and the tales grow taller on down the line.

Don't get me wrong, I'm not saying that the precautions we've taken haven't helped because I believe they have, to a point (and we're way past that point). I'm just saying that Governor Wolf's a clown.

5/31/20

As of Friday, May 29, there were 1,768,868 cases of COVID-19 reported in the United States.

Of those, 103,345 had died and 498,762 had recovered. Does nobody else see the elephant in the room? Are you so blinded by fear that you can't see your noses in front of your faces? The writing on the wall? Other clichés like that? What the hell's going on here?

I'm talking about 1,166,761 poor souls floating around in neither here nor there, locked in an ominous virus-purgatory; not dead, yet not quite alive, either. What's to become of all those disenfranchised folks, riding a train with no apparent destination?

Well, did he ever return?
No he never returned and his fate is still unlearned (what a pity)
He may ride forever 'neath the streets of Boston
He's the man who never returned

And while we're on the subject of reductio ad absurdum, want to know why you have a headache, why you can't sleep at night, why you're gulping down antidepressants by the handful and swilling so much Grey Goose? Here's a clue: On April 17, the Centers for Disease Control and Prevention reported that the total U.S. death rate is below average in 2020. And then on April 29, 12 days later, The Washington Post reported that, "The United States has suffered at least 66,000 more deaths than expected this year."

Huh?

Can we please keep the narrative straight?

Dude?

On January 21, after the first case of COVID-19 was reported in the U.S., Dr. Anthony Fauci, director of the National Institute of Allergy and Infectious Diseases and a member of the Trump administration's coronavirus task force, said, "… [the virus] is not a major threat to the people of the United States, and this is not something that the citizens of the United States right now should be worried about." Then, on April 2, he said, "There should be a national stay-at-home order to combat the spread of the coronavirus." Then on May 12, Dr. Fauci told a Senate committee that the United States could face even more "suffering and death" from COVID-19 if some states rush to open business too early. Then on May 17, he said, "We can't stay locked down for such a considerable period of time that you might do irreparable damage and have unintended consequences, including consequences for health."

Got that?

On March 8, Dr. Fauci said on *60 Minutes* that people don't need masks, that "there's no reason to be walking around with a mask." Then, on May 27, he told CNN that people should be wearing masks, and that he wears one "for people to see that's the kind of thing you should be doing."

Then there's the U.S. Surgeon General, Vice Admiral Jerome M. Adams, saying that wearing face masks does not help you at all when it comes to coronavirus. He tweeted, "Seriously people — STOP BUYING MASKS! They are NOT effective in preventing [the] general public from catching #Coronavirus." Later, he trumpeted the administration's recommendation that everybody should wear masks in public and shared a video explaining how to make your own face masks at home using household items such as T-shirts, scarves and towels.

Apparently, some mask manufacturers are now putting disclaimers on their product that their masks don't prevent COVID-19 because viral particles are so small that they can fit through the masks' material.

Will you please make up your freakin' minds!

Like the CDC saying the virus can be spread on surfaces … no, no, wait, the virus cannot be spread on surfaces … er, easily. Hold the phone — yes it can be spread on surfaces, maybe … for sure. Okay, okay, okay, new research indicates that the virus can and/or cannot be spread on surfaces. That's our story and we're sticking to it.

First you say you do
And then you don't.

And then you say you will
And then you won't.

And while we're on the subject of incongruously hyperbolic contradictions, I've been trying diligently for some time to find data on deaths during the pandemic to compare against historical data, but it's like trying to find Waldo. The best I could come up with are CDC numbers from March 2019 and March 2020 and figure it out for myself. Guess what? My math showed almost 37,000 fewer deaths in March 2020. That may be the result of incomplete reporting, data entry lag time or your business-as-usual incompetency of government bureaucrats.

But perhaps not so strange. USA Today in an article on April 29 stated that over a three-week period, "at least 171,587 people died nationwide — 16,785 deaths more than the historical average. But that number is lower than the 23,460 COVID-19 deaths during the same time period."

Standing on the gallows with my head in a noose. Any minute now I'm expecting all hell to break loose.

Hey, how do you like that: I wrote a whole provocative essay without mentioning Governor Wolf … oh, shit!

6/1/20

According to an article in USA Today, "nearly 90 percent of adult patients hospitalized with COVID-19 in the United States had one or more underlying diseases," and the two leading underlying diseases, by a significant margin, were hypertension and obesity. Other sources have reported similar findings during the coronavirus pandemic.

And here we are, locked down tight, bored and stressed to the max, full of fear over dying or killing Gram and Gramps, while sublimating our anxieties with lots of food (and I use the word "food" here with a touch of irony).

Starting to make sense yet?

Some of the most common causes of high blood pressure are obesity (very symbiotic stuff, eh?), lack of physical activity, too much salt in the diet, too much alcohol consumption and stress. Although in some cases there are contributing medical factors, obesity is primarily caused by eating too much food, especially of the crapola variety.

Starting to make sense yet?

Because we don't want to get or spread COVID-19, we're putting ourselves under tremendous stress, exercising less, drinking too much and stuffing our faces with things full of sugar, salt and fat.

Instant Karma's gonna get you ... pretty soon you're gonna be dead.

You with me? We're fighting a virus that kills about 0.03 percent of the population by contributing to hypertension and obesity in 99.97 percent of the population, and thereby making the other 99.97 percent of the population more vulnerable to the virus we're sacrificing greatly to avoid.

Starting to make sense yet? Does catch-22 ring a bell?

How about, "We have met the enemy and he is us."

I can see clearly now the rain is gone. I can see all obstacles in my way.

I, for one, can testify to the dissipation of quality living through the coronavirus outbreak because it has definitely caused me to break out of most of my clothes. Before the lockdown, my weight was good, I was exercising regularly, generally eating well, getting enough sleep and drinking moderately two or three times a week. Now ... well, that's a different story.

•**Weight:** Fuhgeddaboudit! (That word does keep popping up.) My wardrobe has shrunk to sweatpants, sweatshirts, gym shorts and baggy tees. I can get away with a dress shirt or sport coat for a short period of time and with the right camera angle. Exercise and diet have abandoned me in my hour of need!

•**Exercise:** Pre-meltdown — er, I mean lockdown — I went to the gym an average of five days a week, rode my bike a minimum of 13 miles a day, occasionally hiked and walked every night after dinner. These days, I'm too busy eating. Overall, the problem with the new normal is that it throws everything off balance (and in case you didn't know, we're all — well most of us, anyway — delicately balanced children of the universe). Because of the disruption to my routine and nutrition, my attitude and motivation are under constant attack.

•**Diet:** I used to enjoy the occasional dish of ice cream but tried to avoid my addictions: chocolate and potato chips. Now: What addictions? You mean my new mainstays? Processed sugar, salt, fats and refined carbohydrates are not only bad for the body, but they slow your metabolism and make you feel sluggish. Worse, they negatively affect your psyche, as well. Soul-killing foods not only make you fat, they debilitate your sense of self and put you in the dumps, and the dumps are a hard place to escape. *When you're in a Slump, you're not in for much fun. Un-slumping yourself is not easily done.*

•**Sleep:** Sleep may be the most important element in maintaining good health, but it's probably the most easily affected by the other systems in your daily routine. If you're eating poorly, not getting enough exercise, drinking too much and living under great stress, you'll be lucky to even reach REM sleep. Remember what Shakespeare, George Patton or Vince Lombardi might have said: "Fatigue makes cowards of us all." Fortunately, I could sleep through a nuclear attack, and I do like an afternoon siesta whenever possible, but four or five naps a day is probably too much, do you think?

•**Drinking:** Fuhgeddaboudit! Seriously, fuhgeddaboudit! I'm not talking.

However, I did tell you on Day 19 of Captivity that I was experimenting with a novel cure for the novel virus: Miller Lite. I told you I would keep you posted on my research, and I'm happy to report that it's working; I'm still novel virus-free. I have had to adjust the dosage on occasion, but this is by no means an exact science. I'm still in the experimental stages and expect to be for some time.

I'm also happy to report that I've gotten my weight under control and actually have reversed the trend and lost a few pounds. If we're going back to work in the next couple of weeks, I need to fit into my big-boy clothes, so I'm pulling out all the stops. I'm so proud of myself that I celebrated last night with some fresh strawberries. The only fresh strawberries I could find, though, were stuck to shortcake with whipped cream. During this time of shortages, we all must make sacrifices.

Starting to make sense yet?

6/2/20

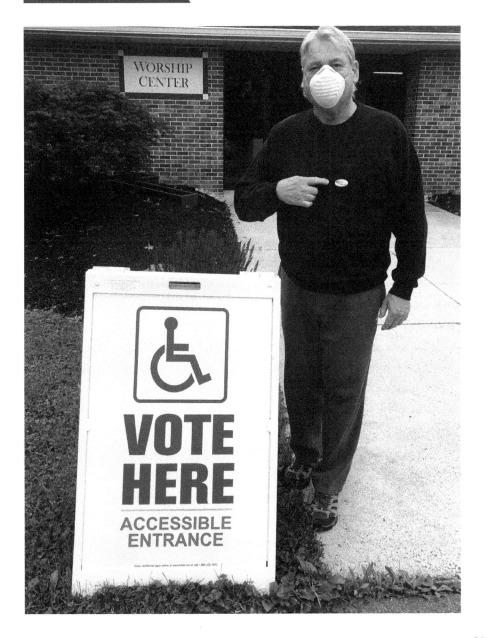

America is pissed off.

Three hundred sixty-five degrees, burning down the house.

This should come as a shock to nobody who watches the news or looks at social media. Or has lived through the pretend social improvements over the past 60 years.

For a few weeks now, it's been apparent that we're sitting on a tinderbox, that most people have been pushed about as far as you can push them without it all blowing up, and when it blows, it's going to expose all the suppressed fear and anger that have been building up for years.

Welcome to the new normal.

And probably the most absurd thing coming out of this lanced boil is being told, "If you want change: Vote."

What a freaking joke! Who are we supposed to vote for, the same old reconstituted and renamed I-want-mine aspirants? Black leaders who show great passion and empathy for their constituents from their multimillion-dollar homes outside the hood? White liberals who bang the drum loudly over inequities and intolerance from their palatial mansions in gated communities? Conservative politicians pontificating on the ersatz, arms-length measures for self-serving, lopsided opportunities from their opulent, walled-off estates? Activists and community leaders extolling the need for fairness and retributive justice from behind their ivy-covered walls? The media lamenting about the inherent injustice of America and the plight of the oppressed from their penthouses and sandcastles in exclusive beach towns?

What a show.

It's like having a car with cancer eating away at the fender, but instead of cutting out the cancer spot and properly repairing it, they keep slapping a new coat of paint over the ever-growing rust and hoping it holds until the next generation shows up.

And then along comes COVID-19, the proverbial straw that broke the camel's back?

Maybe.

Look, the only way to get rid of the malignancies plaguing our great experiment is to change things, not to just keep talking about changing things, or to make a few peripheral changes to make it look like you're changing things, but to actually change things.

And change is hard. Real hard.

But a good start would be to clean up Washington and develop a structure for producing better leaders who are in it for the good of the people, not simply to stroke their fragile egos or line their rapacious pockets. These are a few of my suggestions to accomplish that:

Term Limits: Everybody talks about the weather but nobody does anything about it, right? Well, term limits aren't the weather, and we can do something about them. And we should do something about them! The first thing I'd do is make both the House and Senate four-year terms. Six years for senators is much too long, and two years for representatives is much too short — they spend half that time campaigning. Then I'd make a 12-year limit (three terms) of service in Congress, and not more than two terms in either house.

Compensation: All pay raises for Congress should be equal to raises in Social Security, period. Additionally, pass an amendment that states Congress shall make no laws that do not affect them exactly as they affect the American people, and not some cosmetic, sham crap such as their inclusion in the Affordable Care Act. American politicians have become the greatest snake oil salespeople the world has ever known. It's time to turn off the calliope and shut down the sideshow.

Supreme Court Justices: Let's get rid of the farce. Make it a law that if a justice dies or resigns within a reasonable period of time, perhaps three months, before the end of a President's term, the President and the Senate must replace the justice before the President's term ends. And for Pete's sake, let's institute a mandatory retirement age. Maybe 80 or 85 — no more propping up a body to hold the party's spot on the court.

Campaigning: I propose that nobody running for any office may collect a dime in campaign contributions until the fourth quarter of the year before the election and may not spend any of it until January 1 of the election year. Office holders running for reelection who use taxpayers' time or money to covertly campaign before January 1 will be publicly flogged. It may not be a level playing field for nonincumbents, but any rules, or no rule, will always favor an incumbent — that's why you have to knock out the champ. Further, no corporate donations allowed, only personal donations of not more than $1,000 per person. And best of all, candidates may not collect any money from outside of their districts. Presidential candidates may collect from the entire country, senatorial candidates may collect from their states, but House of Representative candidates may only collect from within the district they propose to represent. And institute a cap on spending. Let's get rid of buying elections.

Post-Service: It should be a law that no person leaving office may be allowed to work for any lobbying group, directly or indirectly, for five years. They should also be excluded from any involvement with domestic or foreign entities doing business with the U.S. government. Let's see how fast the slick pickpockets are willing to serve when they can't devote their lives to getting rich and powerful through politics.

I could go on, but this would be a good start in making fundamentally constructive changes. Of course, it will only happen if everybody starts to take voting more seriously and not dogmatically pull the lever for whomever the party dictates. Quit your ideology — all ideologies are limiting and debilitating, not to mention, extremely impersonal — quit your identity group, quit your voting bloc. Work on being you and being an American, and work for the things that are important to you, not what someone else tells you is supposed to be important to you. Those people always have an agenda, and your welfare is incidental, at best.

Do that and, *Kid, you'll move mountains! Today is your day! Your mountain is waiting. So get on your way!*

Day 80 of Captivity

Let me see if I have this straight: America is moving toward a more inclusive, broad-based government, and the two candidates we have to choose from this fall are old, white guys? One weak and feeble and practically unintelligible; the other unguarded and insolent and practically unintelligible?

You've come a long way, baby!

When Pennsylvanians marched on Harrisburg to protest Governor Wolf's unilateral orders to close businesses and ruin lives, he called the marchers and people who wanted to reopen their businesses to feed their families irresponsible cowards.

When protesters in Philadelphia rioted, destroying businesses and setting fires, Wolf said, "I will continue to work ... to make sure that everyone is able to make their voices heard," regardless of his orders to wear a mask and maintain social distancing, I guess.

Besides the governor being a hypocrite, we learned a couple of things from those messages: Wolfie doesn't seem to care much about businesses not previously (or soon to be again?) owned by him, and he seems to be interested in higher office, being a good soldier and all, regardless of how ridiculous he looks.

But that's probably old news.

It's obligatory for Wolf and his ilk to preface remarks about the riots with the disclaimer, "I don't condone the violence," followed closely by rationalized justification for the violence. I find that kind of sophistry irresponsible and rather cowardly — how about you?

In spite of all that, we here in the Lehigh Valley are all excited about going to Yellow Phase on Friday. Of course, we have no idea what Yellow Phase may be at that time because the governor often changes guidelines based on his soothsayer and horoscope. One of the current guidelines in Yellow Phase is, "STAY AT HOME ORDER LIFTED FOR AGGRESSIVE MITIGATION." (All guidelines are in caps, just so you know he's serious.)

If you're not from Pennsylvania and unaccustomed to Wolf Latin, that means you're supposed to wear a mask unless you're burning down other people's businesses or destroying government property.

The guidelines issued by the state delineating the three phases in nifty shades of red, yellow and green give very little guidance, for purported guidelines. They're vague and incomplete and extremely non-inclusive — nothing about liquor stores or barber shops and hair salons, for example.

Have you seen the guv lately? Not only does he have the awesome power to completely control us, he can control the growth of his own hair because his hair hasn't grown at all during the lockdown. (Not that he has that much, but still.)

What a guy!

> Who's the man among men?
> Who's the super success?
> Don't you know? Can't you guess?
> Ask his fans and his five hangers-on.

When the governor's tea leaves line up properly (while observing aggressive mitigation, of course) and we get to the Green Phase, oh boy, what wonders to appear! Really cool stuff like you can visit prisons but not nursing homes. Why is that, Tommy Boy? Because you so thoroughly infected nursing homes? Or is it that there's nobody left in prison to visit because you gave all the criminals Get Out of Jail Free cards?

I'm particularly fond of the Green Guideline that reads, "PERSONAL RESPONSIBILITY: USE GOOD JUDGMENT, WEAR MASKS AROUND OTHERS, CONTINUE SOCIAL DISTANCING * USE GOOD HEALTH HABITS." When Philadelphia gets to green, that guideline should stop any rioting, for sure. They better be done with it by then, or they'll be in big trouble.

Here's another goodie: "NOT A RETURN TO THE WAY THINGS WERE, BUT CHANGING BEHAVIOR FOR A NEW NORMAL." Apparently ruining businesses, destroying livelihoods, endangering seniors, releasing dangerous criminals from prison and disrupting the lives of millions of people who were in little danger wasn't enough for Ol' Tom. Now he's dictating how we'll live the rest of our lives. What a visionary!

How do you think he does it? I don't know! What makes him so good?

Speaking of good, our dear governor sort of reminds me of Wilson Goode, the former mayor of Philadelphia, who when confronted by the group MOVE (that had killed a cop), announced to the city that he had solved the MOVE problem, "They are moving to New Jersey."

Hey, I just had a thought on how to solve our problems here in PA: Do you think New Jersey will take Tom Wolf?

Last Day of Captivity

6/4/20

We're not gonna take it! No, we ain't gonna take it. We're not gonna take it anymore!

June 5, 2020, probably will not go down in history as anything special (I hope,) but it's a momentous occasion for those of us in the Lehigh Valley still stuck in lockdown. When the clock strikes Friday and the shackles of COVID-19 come off forever (because good luck getting that toothpaste back in the tube), we bid adieu to the Gehenna quarantine and *ease on down, ease on down the road* to freely engage once again in life, liberty and the pursuit of happiness (as long as it doesn't conflict with Governor Wolf's standing guidelines disallowing fun). I would include Philadelphia in this rapture, but they ended their lockdown earlier this week in defiance of Wolf's orders. Remarkably, the governor marched with the protesters in an apparent display of solidarity over the recognition that his edicts over the past three months have been arbitrary and capricious.

The guy is nimble, you must admit.

I have an appointment to get my hair cut on Saturday, and with what I see as blond, but others insist is gray, hair clippings being swept away, so too go 12 weeks that (not to put too fine a point on it) have changed my life forever. Whether it's been changed for the good or for the bad is to be determined.

Stand by.

I'm standing in the wind, but I never wave bye-bye. But I try, I try.

So I'm wrapping up our prodigiously short journey, a roller coaster ride of inexplicable and incongruous twists and turns through a funhouse known as WTF.

Really: WTF!

I bet nobody had in their 2020 New Year's resolutions, "Forget everything you previously knew about civilization and buy lots of toilet paper."

I want to leave you with a thought. Today marks the anniversary of the pro-democracy demonstrations in the streets of Beijing that came to a violent end on this day in 1989, with what is estimated to have cost as many as 1,000 Chinese civilian lives. President George Bush the First did nothing to help the demonstrators or stop the slaughter. It's one of the reasons he was a one-term president who lost to Bill Clinton in 1992.

Had Bush the moxie and integrity to take a stand for the advancement of mankind, China may very well be a different country today and we might not have had to endure the deadly and debilitating coronavirus pandemic.

Who knows?

But what I do know is that we need to find better leaders. All four living, former presidents — Jimmy Carter, Bill Clinton, George Bush the Second and Barack Obama — have weighed in on the current unrest in our country, and all four have, predictably, *as night follows day*, lamented the inequalities behind the riots and proffered the sage wisdom that eradicating those inequities is a most important and sacred mission.

Huh?

Between the four of them, they had 28 years in office, and none of them did a damn thing to eradicate shit. Carter was too busy scolding America while rescue helicopters crashed into each other, Bush was too busy protecting their Arab friends and the oil industry and Clinton and Obama were too busy pontificating on his superior intellect and insulating Wall Street.

Meet the new boss. Same as the old boss. Won't get fooled again, oh no, oh no, no!

DON'T BE FOOLED AGAIN!

So, that's a wrap.

Parting is such sweet sorrow that I shall say goodnight till it be morrow.

But nothing ever really ends, does it? Not as long as we draw breath and carry with us all those people and events that carved us out of possibilities, that forever define who we were, who we are and who we are to be. Where we go from here is enigmatic, as life always is, but hopefully we won't forget where we've been with all its colliding emotions and confusion.

If past is prologue, then our past is exactly who we are, and once we learn to take a firm hold of that, to own it, then we can move past the misunderstandings and misappropriations, the guilt and the anger; once we learn to harness the energy and hope of our inheritance, come to grips with the knowledge that who we were will always be part of who we are, only then can we become one and progress in our inimitable, very American way of diligent and deliberate disagreement. Our past is not our prison, it's our hope.

So we beat on, boats against the current, borne back ceaselessly into the past.

Aftermath

Hugh Jackman tweeted a photo of a police officer hugging a protester and labeled it "solidarity." The cognitively challenged, fanatical misfits went bonkers. As one hatemonger responded, "This is shallow propaganda designed to obfuscate and maintain oppressive dynamics."

We learn two things from this cyber altercation: The first is that Twitter is the devil's workshop, and the second is that the media suck. Okay, we already knew that the media suck, and we had serious suspicions about Twitter. Fox was the only national broadcaster to report this interesting commentary on the world we live in: the incarnation of George Orwell's despotic *1984*. His Ministry of Truth, which dealt solely in misinformation and lies, had nothing on our feckless, bobbing heads who delight in inciting the mob.

How's that for my Q-rating, boss?

It just keeps getting curiouser and curiouser.

A guy I know posted a question on Facebook asking if people knew anybody who had been sick or died from COVID-19. I didn't know all the respondents, but the ones I did created an informative pattern. All the folks I knew who are conservatives didn't know anybody who had been sick or died. All the ones I knew who are liberals knew multiple cases of sickness and death. Wow! All this time we thought the coronavirus was a Chinese/World Health Organization/Left Wing conspiracy, but it turns out to have been a Trump conspiracy all along

This thing is only killing Democrats!

Wake up, America!

They opened the State Stores in the Lehigh Valley on June 5, and I visited my local liquor emporium to pick up some wine. The sidewalk in front of the place was roped off in a kind of cattle chute, sort of like going to the movies. You waited there until you were called to enter through the exit (and it occurred to me, as I waddled in, that being ushered in through the out is probably the best commentary so far on this fascinating odyssey).

I was told to pick out what I wanted. I selected a couple of bottles that I removed from the shelves with my bare hands and took them to the plastic encaged checkout counter. I was instructed to hand the bottles through a small opening in the shield, one at a time, from my bare hands to the bare hands of the cashier, who proceeded to scan the bottles, one at time, and bag them separately, with her bare hands. I was then ordered (this not having to think about anything is really quite liberating) to hold up my credit card so the cashier could read the numbers and punch them into the credit card keypad. What a good idea, not letting me touch the keypad … with my bare hands.

Our state is so smart!

Not too far from where I live, two men were waiting in line at a drugstore, one wearing a mask and one not wearing a mask. The one wearing a mask got in the unmasked face of the other guy for not wearing a mask, and the guy not wearing a mask got right back in the face of the guy wearing a mask. The argument turned into a confrontation that turned into a fistfight in the parking lot.

Both men were arrested, thus continuing the distracting debate over whether it's safer to wear a mask or not wear a mask.

Meanwhile, I finally got my hair cut and immediately lost three pounds (speaking of liberating experiences). We filmed the excavation and used it as part of the promotional package to support this book. It's available on my YouTube channel — Richard Plinke — if you're interested, and if so, I have some advice: Get a life!

Before I go, I would be remiss in not thanking my greatest inspiration for writing this book, Governor Tom Wolf of Pennsylvania. He gave me so much material and made such a great foil. For those of you not from the Keystone State, Wolf represented to me the epitome of the overwrought silliness that plagued us during the plague.

As for me, time to get back to selling the plague.

Acknowledgments

This is the part of the book where I get to thank the folks who've helped me get it into your hands. You may want to thank them, too … or not. Before I do, though, I have a tradition of recognizing an individual with a special de-acknowledgment for his contribution to the great Philistine tradition of myopic obtuseness.

I wrote a monthly column in Lehigh Valley Business for seven years and developed a pretty good following. I had a great relationship with the publisher and editor. I also picked up some business leads from the exposure those pieces afforded me, not to mention a lot of that writing went into my first three books. Unfortunately, the company that owned the paper was sold a couple of years ago, and the publisher and editor were downsized out the door — thank you very much for doing such a great job building the paper into a valuable asset that could be sold for gobs of moolah. Don't let the door hit you in the … well, you know how it goes.

The new editor was Joel Berg, a man I never met, but the exchange of a couple of emails told me all I needed to know about him. The first piece I sent in under his watch was 1,300 words long. He asked me to trim it to 750 words. I was used to being asked to keep my stuff at around 800 words, but I when I get going …

After I reworked it, I sent it back with this comment: "I trimmed the piece to 995 words, and I believe that's as much as can be done without losing its viability and flow. In my defense, the previous editors gave me some leeway on size primarily because of the reasons stated above: viability and flow."

Mr. Berg responded, "I grew up reading Art Buchwald in the

Washington Post, a writer whose regular columns were witty, full of life and rarely over 750 words. And they always told a good story. And many jokes get through a set-up, payoff and close in less than 200 words (Knock Knock). I plan on sticking to the original length requirement. Thanks for understanding."

Understanding?

Yeah, I understand! You just compared my writing to a knock-knock joke!

I never submitted another piece to the journal, and Mr. Berg was gone a couple of months later.

Don't let the door hit you in the ... oh, it can hit you anywhere and still make sense.

My wife, Terry, and our sons, Patrick and Daniel, took all the pictures in this book, not necessarily with great enthusiasm.

As always, I want to thank my good friend John Hayes for reading my stuff and telling me it's good. Sometimes he tells me it's bad, but I ignore that kind of myopic obtuseness.

One more shout out to Melissa Draving and Deb Colitas for inspiring me to write this book. (And another mention can't hurt me in the couple-of-extra-free-hours-department, can it?)

Jennifer Bright, my publisher, is very bright. Thank God.

Dina Hall did her usual excellent job on the book jacket design, and photog Patrick Shuck added the terrific cover picture, along with bailing me out of quicksand with my low-resolution iPhone pictures.

Bill Kline is a true professional editor who's a joy to work with, and editor Kerry Boderman made my writing better, as she always does.

Brenda Lange, my longtime enabler, pushed me into putting these provocative essays into book form. Blame her.

Bibliography of Unattributed Quotations

Introduction
• You want the truth? You can't handle the truth! — *A Few Good Men*

Day 15 of Captivity
• In my hour of need, etc. — Gilbert O'Sullivan, "Alone Again (Naturally)"

Day 16 of Captivity
• I read the news today, oh boy — John Lennon and Paul McCartney, "A Day in the Life"
• ... the name of the place is I like it like that — Chris Kenner, "I Like It Like That"
• Hey, don't worry, I've been lied to, etc. — The Doobie Brothers, "Minute by Minute"

Day 22 of Captivity
• ... we might as well have a good time — *Animal House*

Day 23 of Captivity
• We're a long way from home. Welcome to the Pleasuredome — Frankie Goes to Hollywood, "Welcome to the Pleasuredome"
• Mine is the last voice that you will ever hear. Do not be alarmed. — Frankie Goes to Hollywood, "Two Tribes"

Day 25 of Captivity
• ... and all the news just repeats itself, like some forgotten dream that we've both seen. —John Prine, "Hello in There"
• sweet songs never last too long on broken radios. — John Prine, Sam Stone
• ... hello in there. — John Prine, "Hello in There"

Day 28 of Captivity
• A sadder man but wiser now I sing these words to you. — Will Holt, "Lemon Tree"
• He said, you must be joking son, where did you get those shoes? — Steely Dan, "Pretzel Logic"

Day 29 of Captivity
• Singing songs and carrying signs. Mostly say, hooray for our side. — Stephen Stills, "For What it's Worth"

Day 30 of Captivity
• Give me a head with hair, long beautiful hair, etc. — James Rado, Gerome Ragni and Galt MacDermot, "Hair (Hair)"
• ... drinking a piña colada at Trader Vic's, and his hair was perfect. — Warren Zevon, LeRoy Marinell and Waddy Wachtel, "Werewolves of London"

Day 36 of Captivity
• Sometimes you feel like a nut, sometimes you don't. — Leo Corday and Leon Carr, an advertising jingle for The Peter Paul Candy Manufacturing Co.'s Almond Joy and Mounds
• I thought by now you'd realize, there ain't no way to hide your lyin' eyes. — Don Henley and Glenn Frey, "Lyin' Eyes"
• ... look what's happening out in the street: Got a revolution, got to revolution! — Marty Balin and Paul Kantner, "Volunteers"

Day 39 of Captivity
• Helter skelter, helter skelter, helter skelter! — John Lennon and Paul McCartney, "Helter Skelter"
• When logic and proportion have fallen sloppy dead. — Grace Slick, "White Rabbit"
• "Curiouser and curiouser!" cried Alice. — Lewis Carroll, *Alice's Adventures in Wonderland*

Day 42 of Captivity
• I'll be seeing you, In all the old familiar places, etc. — Sammy Fain and Irving Kahal, "I'll Be Seeing You"
• Ain't that good news? Man ain't that news? — Sam Cooke, "Ain't That Good News"

Day 44 of Captivity
• Everybody's talking at me. I don't hear a word they're saying — Fred Neil, "Everybody's Talkin'"
• Whatayatalk, whatayatalk, whatayatalk, whatayatalk, whatayatalk? — Meredith Willson, "Rock Island (The Music Man)"

Day 46 of Captivity
• And when I awoke I was alone. This bird had flown. — John Lennon and Paul McCartney, "Norwegian Wood"

- In every life we have some trouble, but when you worry you make it double. Don't worry, be happy. — Bobby McFerrin, "Don't Worry, Be Happy"

Day 51 of Captivity
- Come on and let the good times roll. We're gonna stay here till we soothe our souls. — Sam Cooke, "Good Times"
- ... hairy noon and night, hair that's a fright, etc.; bangled, tangled, spangled — Gerome Ragni, James Rado and Galt MacDermot, "Hair (Hair)"
- Master of the house. Keeper of the zoo. Ready to relieve 'em of a sou or two. — Claude-Michel Schönberg, Alain Boublil, Jean-Marc Natel and Herbert Kretzmer, "Master of the House (Les Misérables)"

Day 53 of Captivity
- ... green-eyed ladies, lovely ladies — Jerry Corbetta, J.C. Phillips and David Riordan, "Green Eyed Lady"

Day 57 of Captivity
- Nobody told me there'd be days like these. Strange days indeed. — strange days indeed. — John Lennon, "Nobody Told Me"
- Clowns to the left of me, jokers to the right; here I am, stuck in the middle with you. — Stealers Wheel, "Stuck in the Middle with You"

Day 59 of Captivity
- Things they do look awful c-c-cold — talkin', etc. — The Who, My Generation
- ... caught the last train for the coast — Don McLean, "American Pie"
- Living in the U.S.A. Somebody give me a cheeseburger. — Steve Miller, "Living in the U.S.A."
- I'm going on down to Yasgur's farm, etc. — Joni Mitchell, "Woodstock"

Day 60 of Captivity
- Say goodbye to Hollywood. Say goodbye my baby. — Billy Joel, "Say Goodbye to Hollywood"
- We all have a face that we hide away forever — Billy Joel, "The Stranger"
- Mama, if that's movin' up then I'm movin' out. — Billy Joel, "Movin' Out'
- ... come on, babe, and take me away. We got some money to spend tonight. — Billy Joel, "Weekend Song"

Day 64 of Captivity
- All this whinin' and cryin' and pitchin' a fit, etc. — Eagles, "Get Over It"
- Trouble ahead, trouble behind, etc. — Grateful Dead, "Casey Jones"
- I wish that I knew what I know now. — Ronnie Lane and Ronnie Wood, 'Ooh La La"

- Up ahead in the distance, I saw a shimmering light. — Eagles, "Hotel California"
- You put your head in. You put your head out. — Governor Tom Wolf, "Principals of Government"

Day 71 of Captivity
- Well here's another clue for you all, etc. — John Lennon and Paul McCartney, "Glass Onion"
- Expert, texpert choking smokers, etc. — John Lennon and Paul McCartney, "I am the walrus"

Day 72 of Captivity
- 'Cause if my eyes don't deceive me, etc. — Joe Jackson, "Is She Really Going Out with Him"
- I don't care too much for money, etc. — John Lennon and Paul McCartney, "Can't Buy Me Love"
- ... the heaviest cat, the heaviest cat you ever did see. — Donald Storball, "Cool Jerk"
- Don't throw the past away, etc. — Peter Allen and Carole Bayer Sager, "Everything Old is New Again"

Day 73 of Captivity
- Casey would waltz with the strawberry blonde, etc. — John Palmer and Charles Wardy, "And the Band Played On"
- Got to give us what we want, etc. — Chuck D and Eric Sadler, "Fight the Power"

Day 74 of Captivity
- Send in the clowns, etc. — Stephen Sondheim, "Send in the Clowns"
- But I know the neighborhood, etc. — Gary Richrath, "Take It on the Run"

Day 77 of Captivity
- Well, did he ever return, etc. — Jacqueline Steiner and Bess Lomax Hawes, "M.T.A."
- First you say you do, etc. — Sid Robin and Charlie Shavers, "Undecided"

Day 78 of Captivity
- Instant Karma's gonna get you, etc. — John Lennon, Instant Karma
- I can see clearly now the rain is gone, etc. — Johnny Nash, "I Can See Clearly Now"
- When you're in a Slump, you're not in for much fun, etc. — Dr. Seuss, *Oh, The Places You'll Go!*

Day 79 of Captivity
- Three hundred sixty-five degrees, etc. — David Byrne and Chris Frantz, "Burning Down the House"
- Kid, you'll move mountains!, etc. — Dr. Seuss, *Oh, The Places You'll Go!*

Day 80 of Captivity
- Who's the man among men?, etc. — Josh Gad and Luke Evans, Gaston (*Beauty and the Beast*)
- How do you think he does it?, etc. — Pete Townshend, "Pinball Wizard "

Last Day of Captivity
- We're not gonna take it, etc. — Dee Snider, "We're Not Gonna Take It"
- ... ease on down, ease on down the road — Charles Smalls, "Ease on Down the Road (*The Wiz*)"
- I'm standing in the wind, etc. — David Bowie, "Modern Love"
- ... as night follows day, — William Shakespeare, *Hamlet*
- Meet the new boss, etc. — Pete Townshend, "Won't Get Fooled Again"
- Parting is such sweet sorrow, etc. — William Shakespeare, *Romeo and Juliet*
- So we beat on, boats against the current, etc. — F. Scott Fitzgerald, *The Great Gatsby*

CPSIA information can be obtained
at www.ICGtesting.com
Printed in the USA
BVHW060455310820
587631BV00005B/39

9 780988 876422